Social Studies

myWorld
ACTIVITY GUIDE
5

SAVVAS
LEARNING COMPANY

ISBN-13: 978-0-328-97318-7
ISBN-10:   0-328-97318-1

9   20

Contents

Chapter 8

Chapter 9

Graphic Organizers

myWorld Activity Guide

How to Use This Book

The *myWorld Activity Guide* was designed for teachers who love social studies but want to teach it in a different way. The program focuses on key topics in social studies, aligning to content frequently taught in each grade from kindergarten to Grade 5. The chapters in this book introduce students to social studies through fun activities and engaging inquiries. You can use the Activity Guide on its own, with associated support materials, or in connection with your basal program.

Teacher Planner

The Chapter Planner outlines the chapter's content in a clear chart with this information:

- **Description** gives a quick overview of each activity and its steps

- **Duration** offers a time estimate, making it easy to plan

- **Materials** lists the materials you will need for each part of the lesson

- **Participants** suggests whether to complete each part of the activity as whole class, small group, or individual

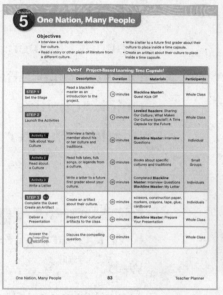

Quest

Each chapter includes detailed lesson suggestions for a long-term inquiry, or Quest.

- Each Quest starts with a Compelling Question, designed to engage students in the inquiry.

- The Quest is set up with three steps: Set the Stage, Launch the Activities, and Complete the Quest.

- Within each step, you'll find suggestions for guiding students to complete a series of activities, culminating in a final product, such as a hands-on project, presentation, civic discussion, or writing project.

- Each chapter contains suggestions for modifying the activities for English Learners.

- Where appropriate, student worksheets are provided to support student completion of the Quest.

- Rubrics in the front of the book will help you and your students evaluate their work.

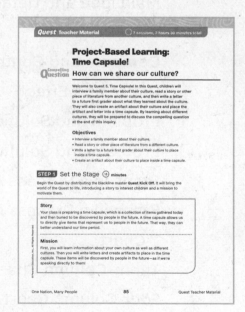

Quick Activities

Each chapter includes detailed lesson suggestions for a series of short activities related to the chapter content. Where appropriate, student worksheets are provided to support student completion of activities. Rubrics in the front of this book will help you and your students evaluate their work on each activity. The Activity Guide also offers suggestions for modifying the activities for English Learners.

Examples of Quick Activities are:

Games   Preparing and Acting Out a Skit

Debates   Building a Social Media Profile

Art Projects   Map Activities

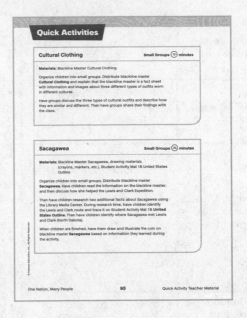

Read Aloud or Readers Theater

Each chapter has a Read Aloud or Readers Theater related to chapter content. With grade-appropriate language, the stories and Readers Theaters bring to life important content related to the chapter.

Graphic Organizers

You will find a wide variety of graphic organizers at the back of this book. You will find many uses for them as your students complete the activities and Quests described in this book.

How to Use This Book

Opinion Writing

Directions: Copy the rubric for individuals or groups (for collaborative writing projects). Rank individuals or groups for each skill.

	4 Excellent	3 Good	2 Satisfactory	1 Needs Improvement
Introduce the topic or text.	• The topic is clearly introduced and is accurate.	• The topic is introduced and is mostly accurate.	• An attempt is made to introduce the topic, but it is incorrect and/or unclear.	• The topic is not introduced.
State an opinion.	• An opinion is clearly stated and accurately responds to the topic.	• An opinion that mostly responds to the topic is stated but is vague.	• An attempt is made to state an opinion, but it does not respond to the topic and/or is unclear.	• An opinion is not stated.
Provide reasons that support the opinion.	• More than one reason that clearly supports the opinion is provided. • All provided reasons are supported with facts and details. (Grades 4–5)	• Only one reason is provided or more than one reason is provided, but the reasons mostly support the opinion. (Grade 3) • Provided reasons are mostly supported with facts and details. (Grades 4–5)	• An attempt is made to provide a reason, but the reason is either unclear or does not support the opinion. (Grade 3) • Facts and details do not clearly support the provided reasons. (Grades 4–5)	• No reasons are provided. (Grade 3) • Provided reasons are not supported with facts or details. (Grades 4–5)
Use linking words and phrases to connect opinion and reasons.	• Linking words and phrases consistently are used correctly to connect the opinion and reasons.	• Linking words and phrases are generally used correctly to connect the opinion and reasons.	• Linking words and phrases are used incorrectly to connect the opinion and reasons.	• Linking words and phrases are not used to connect the opinion and reasons.
Provide a concluding statement or section.	• A concluding statement or section is provided and includes a clear restatement of the opinion without introducing new ideas. (Grade 3) • A concluding statement or section is provided that clearly relates to the opinion without introducing new ideas. (Grades 4–5)	• A concluding statement or section is provided, but it includes a vague restatement of the opinion or introduces new ideas. (Grade 3) • A concluding statement or section is provided that generally relates to the opinion or introduces new ideas. (Grades 4–5)	• An attempt is made to provide a concluding statement or section, but it includes a vague restatement of the opinion and new ideas. (Grade 3) • A concluding statement or section is provided that vaguely relates to the opinion and introduces new ideas. (Grades 4–5)	• A concluding statement or section is not provided.

Informative/Explanatory

Directions: Copy the rubric for individuals or groups (for collaborative writing projects). Rank individuals or groups for each skill.

	4 Excellent	**3** Good	**2** Satisfactory	**1** Needs Improvement
Introduce a topic.	• The topic is clearly introduced and is accurate.	• The topic is introduced and is mostly accurate.	• An attempt is made to introduce the topic but is incorrect and/or unclear.	• The topic is not introduced.
Group related information together.	• Related information is clearly and consistently grouped together.	• Related information is mostly grouped together.	• Related information is sometimes grouped together, but organization of other information is unclear.	• Related information is not grouped together.
Develop the topic with facts, definitions, and details.	• Consistently provides facts, definitions, and details to develop the topic.	• Generally provides facts, definitions, and details to develop the topic.	• Gives some facts, definitions, and details, but they are inaccurate or have a vague link to the topic.	• No information, facts, or definitions are provided.
Use linking words and phrases to connect ideas within categories of information.	• Linking words and phrases consistently are used correctly to connect ideas within categories of information.	• Linking words and phrases are generally used correctly to connect ideas within categories of information.	• Linking words and phrases are used incorrectly to connect ideas within categories of information.	• Linking words and phrases are not used to connect ideas within categories of information.
Provide a concluding statement or section.	• A concluding statement or section is provided and includes a clear restatement of the topic without introducing new ideas. (Grade 3) • A concluding statement or section is provided that clearly relates to the information or explanation presented without introducing new ideas. (Grades 4–5)	• A concluding statement or section is provided, but it includes a vague restatement of the topic or introduces new ideas. (Grade 3) • A concluding statement or section is provided that generally relates to the information or explanation presented or introduces new ideas. (Grades 4–5)	• An attempt is made to provide a concluding statement or section, but it includes a vague restatement of the topic and new ideas. (Grade 3) • A concluding statement or section is provided that vaguely relates to the information or explanation presented and introduces new ideas. (Grades 4–5)	• A concluding statement or section is not provided.

Narrative Writing

Directions: Copy the rubric for individuals or groups (for collaborative writing projects). Rank individuals or groups for each skill.

	4 Excellent	3 Good	2 Satisfactory	1 Needs Improvement
Establish a situation and introduce a narrator and/or characters.	• The situation and the narrator and/or characters are clearly established.	• The situation and the narrator and/or characters are somewhat established.	• The situation and the narrator and/or characters are established but are vague.	• The situation and the narrator and/or characters are not established.
Organize an event sequence that unfolds naturally.	• The event sequence is organized so that it unfolds naturally.	• The event sequence is mostly organized so that it unfolds naturally.	• The event sequence is somewhat organized, but the events unfold awkwardly.	• The event sequence is not organized.
Use dialogue and descriptions to develop experiences and events.	• Dialogue and descriptions are used to clearly and effectively develop experiences and events.	• Some dialogue and descriptions are used to develop experiences and events.	• Dialogue and descriptions are used to develop experiences and events but are vague.	• No dialogue and descriptions are used to develop experiences and events.
Use temporal words and phrases to signal event order. (Grade 3)	• Temporal words and phrases are used consistently and accurately to signal event order.	• Temporal words and phrases are sometimes used to accurately signal event order.	• Temporal words and phrases are occasionally used to signal event order and/or are used inaccurately.	• Temporal words and phrases are not used.
Use a variety of transitional words and phrases to manage the sequence of events. (Grades 4–5)	• A variety of transitional words and phrases are used consistently and accurately to manage the sequence of events.	• A variety of transitional words and phrases are sometimes used to accurately manage the sequence of events.	• Transitional words and phrases are occasionally used to manage the sequence of events and may be used inaccurately or repetitively.	• Transitional words and phrases are not used to manage the sequence of events.
Use concrete words and phrases and sensory details to convey experiences and events. (Grades 4–5)	• Concrete words and phrases and sensory details are used consistently and accurately to convey experiences and events.	• Concrete words and phrases and sensory details are sometimes used to accurately convey experiences and events.	• Concrete words and phrases and sensory details are occasionally used to convey experiences and events and may be used inaccurately or repetitively.	• Concrete words and phrases and sensory details are not used to convey experiences and events.
Provide a sense of closure. (Grade 3)	• A strong sense of closure is provided with a clear ending.	• A sense of closure is provided with a vague ending.	• An attempt is made to provide closure with an ending that trails off.	• A sense of closure is not provided.
Provide a conclusion that follows from the narrated experiences or events. (Grades 4–5)	• A conclusion that clearly follows from the narrated experiences or events is provided.	• A conclusion that mostly follows from the narrated experiences or events is provided.	• A conclusion that loosely follows from the narrated experiences or events is provided.	• A conclusion that follows from the narrated experiences or events is not provided.

Project-Based Learning

Directions: Copy the rubric for individuals or groups. Rank individuals or groups for each skill as they conduct research to complete an inquiry project.

	4 Excellent	3 Good	2 Satisfactory	1 Needs Improvement
PLAN THE INQUIRY: Collaborate to develop a project plan.	• Assigns and accepts tasks within the group, encouraging all group members to play a role and contribute equally. • Engages effectively in collaborative discussions about the inquiry for the duration of the project by explicitly building on others' ideas and expressing their own clearly. • Participates fully in identifying details of the final outcome.	• Accepts tasks within the group, generally encouraging group members to play a role and contribute equally. • Engages in collaborative discussions about the inquiry by building on others' ideas and expressing their own. • Participates in identifying the details for the final outcome.	• Sometimes accepts tasks within the group, occasionally encouraging group members to play a role and contribute equally. • Sometimes engages in collaborative discussions about the inquiry by attempting to build on others' ideas and mostly expressing their own. • Participates somewhat in identifying the details for the final outcome.	• Rarely accepts tasks within the group or encourages group members to play a role and contribute equally. • Rarely engages in collaborative discussions about the inquiry, does not build on others' ideas, and rarely expresses their own. • Does not participate in identifying the details for the final outcome.
DO YOUR RESEARCH. Find sources to support your inquiry.	• Finds relevant evidence in support of own interpretations. • Routinely asks and answers questions, referring to the text to clarify meaning. • Reads or explores a number of sources to gain, modify, or extend knowledge or to learn different perspectives. • Always synthesizes and draws conclusions from information acquired through research.	• Generally finds relevant evidence in support of own interpretations. • Usually asks and answers questions, referring to the text to clarify meaning. • Reads or explores at least one source to gain, modify, or extend knowledge or to learn different perspectives. • Generally synthesizes and draws conclusions from information acquired through research.	• Finds some evidence in support of own interpretations, but some may be irrelevant. • Occasionally asks and answers questions, referring to the text to clarify meaning. • Attempts to read or explore sources but struggles to gain, modify, or extend knowledge. • Attempts to synthesize and draw conclusions from information acquired through research, but conclusions are vague or inaccurate.	• Finds little or no evidence in support of own interpretations. • Rarely or never asks and answers questions or refers to the text to clarify meaning. • Does not attempt to read or explore sources to gain, modify, or extend knowledge. • Does not synthesize or draw conclusions from information acquired through research.
PRODUCE THE PRODUCT: Demonstrate understanding of key ideas.	• Expresses and refines understanding of new concepts while creating the product. • Consistently uses language acquired from research in speaking and writing about the product. • Adds multiple visuals or multimedia components to enhance the product.	• Generally expresses and refines understanding of new concepts while creating the product. • Generally uses language acquired from research in speaking and writing about the product. • Adds at least one visual or multimedia to enhance the product.	• Occasionally expresses and refines understanding of new concepts while creating the product. • Occasionally uses language acquired from research in speaking and writing about the product. • Adds a visual or multimedia, but it is irrelevant and does not enhance the product.	• Rarely expresses and refines understanding of new concepts while creating the product. • Rarely uses language acquired from research in speaking and writing about the product. • Does not include a visual or multimedia.
REFLECT ON THE INQUIRY: Discuss the Compelling Question.	• Fully articulates a meaningful response to the Compelling Question.	• Generally articulates a meaningful response to the Compelling Question.	• Attempts to articulate a response to the Compelling Question, but the response is vague or irrelevant.	• Does not attempt to respond to the Compelling Question.

Collaborative Discussion

Directions: Copy the rubric for individuals, pairs, or groups as they engage in collaborative discussions with diverse partners about grade-appropriate topics and texts, including discussions about current local, national, and international issues. Rank individuals or groups for each skill.

	4 Excellent	3 Good	2 Satisfactory	1 Needs Improvement
Come to discussions prepared.	• Reads/studies all discussion materials prior to discussion. • Explicitly uses information and advance preparation to explore ideas during discussion.	• Reads/studies most discussion materials prior to discussion. • Mostly uses information and advance preparation to explore ideas during discussion.	• Reads/studies some discussion materials prior to discussion. • Occasionally uses information and advanced preparation to explore ideas during discussion.	• Reads/studies little if any discussion materials prior to discussion. • Does not use information and advanced preparation to explore ideas during discussion.
Follow agreed-upon rules for discussions.	• Follows agreed-upon rules at all times. • Carries out all assigned roles. (G4–5) • Consistently uses deliberative processes when making group decisions.	• Follows agreed-upon rules most of the time. • Carries out most assigned roles. (G4–5) • Generally uses deliberative processes when making group decisions.	• Follows agreed-upon rules but needs occasional direction. • Carries out some assigned roles with direction and reminders. (G4–5) • Sometimes uses deliberative processes when making group decisions.	• Does not follow agreed-upon rules without teacher direction. • Does not carry out assigned roles. (G4–5) • Does not use deliberative processes when making group decisions.
Pose and respond to specific questions to clarify or follow up on information.	• Uses questions and responses that explicitly clarify or follow up on the information presented and purposefully contributes to the discussion. • Poses questions that clearly link to the remarks of others.	• Uses questions and responses that generally clarify or follow up on the information presented and contributes to the discussion. • Poses questions that mostly link to the remarks of others.	• Attempts to use questions and responses that clarify or follow up on the information presented and attempts to contribute to the discussion. • Poses questions that vaguely link to the remarks of others.	• Does not use questions or responses that clarify or follow up on the information presented and does not contribute to the discussion. • Does not pose questions that link to the remarks of others.
Report on a topic.	• Thoroughly explains ideas and understanding in light of the discussion. • Expresses key ideas clearly. (G4–5) • Always provides facts that are appropriate to the discussion and details that are descriptive and relevant. • Always speaks clearly at an understandable pace. • Consistently raises reasons and evidence supporting particular points. (G4–5)	• Mostly explains ideas and understanding in light of the discussion. • Generally expresses key ideas clearly. (G4–5) • Usually provides facts that are appropriate to the discussion and details that are descriptive and relevant. • Generally speaks clearly at an understandable pace. • Mostly raises reasons and evidence supporting particular points. (G4–5)	• Attempts to explain ideas and understanding in light of the discussion. • Occasionally expresses key ideas, but they may not be clear. (G4–5) • Provides facts and details, but some facts and details may not be descriptive or relevant. • Attempts to speak clearly at an understandable pace but is difficult to understand at times. • Occasionally raises reasons and evidence, but these do not always support particular points. (G4–5)	• Rarely explains ideas and understanding in light of the discussion. • Rarely if ever expresses key ideas. (G4–5) • Does not provide facts or details. • Does not speak clearly or at an understandable pace. • Rarely if ever raises reasons and evidence supporting particular points. (G4–5)

Readers Theater/Read Aloud

Directions: Copy the rubric for individuals or groups. Rank individuals or groups for each skill.

	4 Excellent	3 Good	2 Satisfactory	1 Needs Improvement
BEFORE READING: Research and practice part.	• Plans own part and practices reading aloud with correct projection and diction. • Consistently uses context to confirm or self-correct word recognition and understanding, rereading as necessary. • Consistently applies grade-level phonics and word analysis skills in decoding words.	• Plans part with some assistance and practices reading aloud with mostly correct projection and diction. • Usually uses context to confirm or self-correct word recognition and understanding. • Usually applies grade-level phonics and word analysis skills in decoding words.	• Attempts to plan own part and practices reading aloud with sometimes incorrect projection and diction. • Occasionally uses context to confirm or self-correct word recognition and understanding. • Sometimes applies grade-level phonics and word analysis skills in decoding words.	• Does not plan own part or practice reading aloud. • Rarely if ever uses context to confirm or self-correct word recognition or understanding. • Rarely if ever applies grade-level phonics and word analysis skills in decoding words.
WHILE READING ALOUD OR PERFORMING: Communicate meaning with clear use of language and enthusiastic delivery.	• Consistently reads text with clear purpose and understanding, speaking clearly at an understandable pace. • Consistently reads prose orally with accuracy, appropriate rate, and expression on successive readings to support comprehension. • Understands the movement in front of a group, consistently maintains appropriate eye contact.	• Generally reads text with clear purpose and understanding, usually speaking clearly at an understandable pace. • Generally reads prose orally with accuracy, appropriate rate, and expression on successive readings to support comprehension. • Usually understands the movement in front of a group; usually maintains appropriate eye contact.	• Attempts to read text with purpose and understanding but sometimes does not speak clearly or at an understandable pace. • Reads prose orally but there are a few errors in accuracy, rate, and/or expression, even on successive readings. • Sometimes understands the movement in front of a group; attempts to maintain appropriate eye contact.	• Does not read text with clear purpose or understanding. • Does not read prose orally with accuracy, appropriate rate, or expression, even on successive readings. • Does not understand the movement in front of a group or maintain eye contact.
AFTER READING: Ask and answer questions about a reading of a text.	• Consistently asks clear questions related to the topic to check their own understanding of information presented. • Always links comments to the remarks of others. • Consistently offers appropriate elaboration and details.	• Often asks questions related to the topic to check their own understanding of information presented. • Often links comments to the remarks of others. • Often offers appropriate elaboration and details.	• Occasionally asks questions related to the topic to check their own understanding of information presented. • Occasionally links comments to the remarks of others. • Occasionally offers elaboration and details but may not be appropriate to the topic.	• Rarely if ever asks questions related to the topic to check their own understanding of information presented. • Rarely if ever links comments to the remarks of others. • Rarely if ever offers elaboration and details.
AFTER READING: Demonstrate comprehension of text.	• Accurately determines the main ideas and supporting details of a text read aloud. • Clearly distinguishes between own point of view and that of the narrator or characters.	• Usually determines the main ideas and supporting details of a text read aloud accurately. • Generally distinguishes between own point of view and that of the narrator or characters.	• Sometimes determines the main ideas and supporting details of a text read aloud but is not always accurate. • Has difficulty with distinguishing between own point of view and that of the narrator or characters.	• Rarely if ever determines the main ideas and supporting details of a text read aloud. • Is unable to distinguish between own point of view and that of the narrator or characters.

Chapter 1

The First Americans

Objectives

- Describe how geography and climate influenced the lives of various American Indian groups.
- Identify how the natural environment influenced the customs and folklore traditions of the American Indians.
- Explore how environment impacts present-day life.

Quest Project-Based Learning: How the First Americans Used Land

	Description	Duration	Materials	Participants
STEP 1 Set the Stage	Read a blackline master as an introduction to the project.	15 minutes	**Blackline Master:** Quest Kick Off	Whole Class
STEP 2 Launch the Activities	Watch a video with background information.	5 minutes	**Video:** Ancient Farmers: Builders in Stone, **Leveled Readers:** The First Americans: American Indians; The Nations of North America; A History of American Indian Nations	Whole Class
Activity 1 The Natural Environments of Yesterday	Describe the geography and land of pre-Columbian natural environments.	30 minutes	Three-Column Chart graphic organizer, **Student Activity Mat:** 3A Graphic Organizer classroom or Library Media Center resources	Small Groups
Activity 2 The Impact of Land and Geography	Gather information about how geography affected the way of life for American Indian groups.	45 minutes	Three-Column Chart graphic organizer or **Student Activity Mat:** 3A Graphic Organizer, classroom or Library Media Center resources	Small Groups
Activity 3 Prepare to Create	Gather materials and resources, outline plan, and write description of mural.	45 minutes	Completed Quest materials, sticky notes, large sheets of paper	Small Groups
Activity 4 Land and Geography Today	Determine the impact land and geography has on people today.	20 minutes	Completed Quest materials	Small Groups
STEP 3 ELL Complete the Quest Create a Mural	Create a mural that shows how American Indian groups used the land.	45 minutes	Annotated paper from Activity 3, completed Quest materials, various art supplies, scissors, glue/glue sticks	Small Groups
Answer the Compelling **Q**uestion	Discuss the compelling question.	15 minutes		Whole Class

Quick Activities

	Description	Duration	Materials	Participants
Foods and Goods	Identify how environment impacted what the American Indian groups ate and the goods they produced.	25 minutes	Classroom or Library Media Center resources	Partners
Let's Barter!	Simulate a barter system in the classroom.	15 minutes	Index cards	Whole Class
American Indian Groups and Religion	Read about American Indian beliefs.	20 minutes	Classroom or Library Media Center resources	Individual
How Does Where I Live Influence My Local Government?	Identify possible government responsibilities related to geography.	20 minutes	Classroom or Library Media Center resources	Partners
Read Aloud: ELL American Indian Legends	Read aloud American Indian folk tales about the natural world.	20 minutes	Read Aloud pages	Small Groups

Project-Based Learning: How the First Americans Used Land

Q Compelling Question How has land use changed over time?

Welcome to Quest 1, How the First Americans Used Land. In this Quest, your students will create a mural that illustrates how pre-Columbian American Indian groups were affected by geography and how they used the land. Through their study of pre-Columbian American Indian groups' customs, traditions, economies, and systems of government, students will be prepared to discuss the compelling question at the end of this inquiry.

Objectives

- Describe how geography and climate influenced the lives of various American Indian groups.
- Identify how the natural environment influenced the customs and traditions of the American Indians.
- Explore how environment impacts present-day life.

STEP 1   Set the Stage   ⏱ 15 minutes

Begin the Quest by distributing the blackline master **Quest Kick Off.** It will bring the world of the Quest to life, introducing a story to interest students and a mission to motivate them.

Story

Your town wants to honor the first Americans who lived in the area. Town leaders are looking for students to create a mural that will help the people remember and learn from the Indian groups.

· ·

Mission

Students have been chosen by members of their community to create a mural that represents the first Americans who once lived in the area.

STEP 2 Launch the Activities

The following four activities will help students prepare for their mission by researching and planning.

Begin by showing the video, **Ancient Farmers: Builders in Stone,** which will give students the content background they need to complete the activities. You may also assign the appropriate Leveled Reader for this chapter.

Divide students into small groups. Assign each small group one of the following American Indian groups:

- cliff dwellers
- pueblo people of the desert Southwest
- American Indians of the Pacific Northwest
- nomadic nations of the Great Plains
- woodland peoples east of the Mississippi River

Activity 1 The Natural Environments of Yesterday   minutes

Materials: Three-Column Chart graphic organizer or **Student Activity Mat:** 3A Graphic Organizer, classroom or Library Media Center resources, colored pencils

Explain to students that the American Indian groups that they have been assigned lived in very different areas and therefore had access to very different environments and resources. Explain that they will be researching and taking notes on these environments.

Distribute the Three-Column Chart graphic organizer or **Student Activity Mat:** 3A: Graphic Organizer, and instruct the students to label the chart and organize the information they gather in three columns in the following manner (each of the headings below should be a heading on one column of the chart):

- Location: Have the students describe where in North America their assigned Indian group lived. Encourage students to describe the location using natural landmarks (e.g., *The Pacific coastal region*).

- Environment: Have the students describe the natural environment of their Indian group. Tell them to include information such as the climate, the type of landforms the group might have had access to, and the primary type of land available to the group (e.g., forest, prairie).

- Resources: In this column, students can describe some of the natural resources that were available to their group (e.g., the types of animals available for hunting, materials used in building or for clothing).

Using classroom or Library Media Center resources, have students look up information about their groups and record it in their charts. When all groups have finished, ask each group to present their research to the class. Encourage the students to take notes during the presentations. Then ask students to consider what their assigned Indian group has in common with other groups, and what makes it unique.

Activity 2 The Impact of Land and Geography 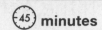 minutes

Materials: Three-Column Chart graphic organizer or **Student Activity Mat:** 3A Graphic Organizer, classroom or Library Media Center resources

In this activity, students will be looking at more ways in which land and geography impacted their assigned Indian group.

Distribute the Three-Column Chart graphic organizer or **Student Activity Mat:** 3A: Graphic Organizer, and have students label the columns "Trade," "Customs," and "Government." Draw a model chart on the board.

Using student input, fill in the chart on the board with information for your state. Ask:

What impact does your state's environment have on trade? (Answers will vary, but should discuss environmental features that are part of your state and it effects trade with other states.)

What impact does the environment have on local customs? (Answers will vary, but should discuss environmental features that are part of your state and how people use it.)

What impact does the environment have on government? (Answers will vary, but should discuss state and local laws and rules that impact or regulate the environment.)

After the class works together to fill out the chart on the board, explain that students should fill in the same kinds of information for their assigned American Indian group. Allow students access to the Library Media Center to find the information they need to fill out their charts.

Materials: Completed Quest materials, sticky notes, large sheets of paper

In this activity, students will be planning their murals using the information that they have collected about their assigned American Indian groups. Present students with examples of murals that show history, culture, or events from the Internet or books. Explain that they can use the examples to inspire their own creative efforts. Remind them that the purpose of their murals is to convey how their assigned American Indian group used geography and land. Model how to analyze one of the examples, emphasizing the function and purpose of murals. Tell students that murals not only demonstrate an artist's talent, but also engage the community, convey important historical events, invite and intrigue the observer, pose significant questions, imply answers, give specific and relevant perspectives, foster conversation, and build connections between the past and present.

Be careful to point out the evidence you would like to see in your students' final products and to support your suggestions with the Project-Based Learning Rubric.

Before they begin, students will need to think about how their American Indian group used the land. This will help them determine the scenes they want to create. Students should outline a plan for their murals.

1. Remind students to focus on the geography, climate, and resources that affected how the group used the land. Have them think about the best way to present their ideas through careful planning.

2. Have groups list at least five ways their assigned Indian group used the land. Have them think about the following questions: Which uses will they portray in the images? Which will they portray in text? What will the images look like? What message and information will the text deliver?

3. Now have groups discuss their plans for how they will create the mural with their group. Help students to divide the tasks evenly between the group members.

4. Distribute the large sheets of paper to each group.

5. Tell students to use sticky notes to mark the large paper. Sticky notes should be placed where they plan to position images and words. Remind students to keep their purpose and audience in mind as they plan.

6. Have students write a draft of the descriptive elements that will accompany their mural.

Materials: Completed Quest materials

Explain to students that they will work together in their groups to discuss the impact of land and geography on their own lives. Have students consider how their local environment impacts them. You can help the groups to think about this by asking questions such as: *How does your region's climate affect the way your community works or plays? How has present-day technology impacted your environment?* Direct students to review their completed Quest materials for ideas. Circulate to help students answer these questions and to facilitate discussion.

Students should take notes on their discussion within their small groups. Then ask each group to talk about their conclusions with the class.

ⓔⓛⓛ Support for English Language Learners

Writing: Explain to students that together, nouns tell who or what a sentence is about and verbs tell how that person, place, thing, or idea behaves or exists. Nouns and verbs generally cannot convey an idea clearly without the help of other words. Adverbs, adverb phrases, and prepositional phrases are examples of word parts that help nouns and verbs make sentences livelier and more interesting. By providing additional details, these word parts help to enhance a sentence's meaning. Provide these examples:

American Indians lived.

American Indians lived in New Jersey.

American Indians lived peacefully in New Jersey.

American Indians lived in New Jersey before any Europeans settled there.

Entering: Help students expand and enrich their sentences. Provide the following basic sentence and help students to expand it: *American Indians hunted bison.* (Possible answer: American Indians hunted huge herds of bison.)

Emerging: Have students apply varied and precise vocabulary and language structures to convey ideas. Provide the sentence: *Cliff dwellers lived in natural caves.* (Possible answer: Cliff dwellers lived in natural caves **that gave them shelter.**)

Developing: Have students work in small groups to apply varied and precise vocabulary and language structures to effectively convey ideas. Have the group expand the following sentence: *American Indians that lived by water _____.* (Possible answer: American Indians that lived by water **ate fish and traveled along the coast.**)

Expanding: Have students apply varied and precise vocabulary and language structures to convey ideas. Have students work in pairs to expand the following sentence: *Nomadic nations hunted _____.* (Possible answer: Nomadic nations hunted **for food to eat.**)

Bridging: Have students construct sentences by applying varied and precise vocabulary and language structures to effectively convey ideas. Ask them to identify the words and phrases that they used to enrich their sentences, providing additional context and information about their group.

STEP 3 Complete the *Quest*

Part 1 Create a Mural minutes

Materials: Annotated paper from Activity 3, completed Quest materials, various art supplies, scissors, glue/glue sticks

Now that students have researched and planned, it is time for them to create their murals. Have students refer to the research they conducted in past activities and to the plan that they made for their mural in Activity 3. Recall their mission of creating and presenting a mural for their town. The mural will honor pre-Columbian American Indians. Remind them to illustrate just how land and geography affected the first Americans' lives by thinking about the colors, symbols, and messages they want to convey. Encourage them to take creative risks but also to accurately convey the information and to consider their audience. Consider inviting an audience of parents, administration, or another class to see the murals and hear students' groups present them. The audience may ask students questions about what they have shown in the mural and how they chose the images and words.

Part 2 Compelling Question (15) minutes

After students create their murals, encourage them to reflect on what they learned. As a class, discuss the compelling question for this Quest, "How has land use changed over time?"

Students have learned about how the environment impacted pre-Columbian American Indian groups. They should think about how environmental factors affect their communities. They should use what they learned to discuss the compelling question.

How the First Americans Used Land

Your town wants to honor the first Americans who lived there. Town leaders are looking for students to create a mural that will help the people remember and learn from the Indian groups. As you prepare to create your murals, you'll research the impact geography had on their way of life, the way their government systems worked, and the customs they developed.

Your Mission

Create a mural that illustrates how your assigned American Indian group used geography and land. Your mural should teach the people of your town about the impact of the natural environment on the first Americans.

To Create a Mural:

Activity 1 **The Natural Environments of Yesterday:** Describe Pre-Columbian geography and resources.

Activity 2 **The Impact of Land and Geography:** Discover the impact of the natural environment on American Indians' ways of life.

Activity 3 **Prepare to Create:** Outline mural plans and write a draft of the descriptions you will use.

Activity 4 **Land and Geography Today:** Analyze the impact of geography and land on your own life.

Complete Your Quest

Create your mural, illustrating the connection between American Indian groups and their natural environment.

Quick Activities

Foods and Goods

Partners 25 minutes

Materials: Classroom or Library Media Center resources

Explain to students that geography determined what foods American Indian groups ate and the goods they produced. Have students work with a partner to select a pre-Columbian American Indian nation that they would like to research. Using classroom or Library Media Center resources, students can study the region of the Indian nation they have chosen to study, and determine the kinds of food they ate and the kinds of goods they produced.

For example, if an Indian group lived near a major waterway such as the Mississippi River, students might find that the group ate large quantities of fish and produced boats for travel.

If time allows, students can perform additional research about American Indian groups and the regions in which they lived, the foods they would have eaten, and the goods and services they produced, or you can allow the partners to present their findings to the class.

Let's Barter!

Whole Class 15 minutes

Materials: Index cards

Explain to students that a barter system is a system in which goods and services are traded, instead of money, to pay for a good or a service. The people trading the good or service assign a value to that good or service and trade for another good or service of equal value. American Indian groups traded with other groups for goods they wanted or needed. For example, Group A may need animal fur for winter clothing from Group B and Group C may need food that Group D grows.

Create a barter system in the classroom by having students draw goods and services on index cards. Have each student use four cards to draw pictures of two goods and two services. Examples of goods might be a video game or pack of their favorite trading cards. Examples of services might be dog walking or baby-sitting.

Then have students circulate in the classroom to find another student with a good or service they want. Once they find a good or service they want, have them see if the other student is willing to trade for one of their goods or services.

For example, if one student is offering a baby-sitting service and another student has a younger sibling, those students may be able to come to an agreement. Tell students that depending on the value placed on a good or service, students may expect to trade two items for one.

American Indian Groups and Religion

Individual ⟨20⟩ minutes

Materials: Classroom or Library Media Center resources

Arrange for students to visit the Library Media Center to select a book about American Indian groups and their religious beliefs. If possible, ask the school librarian to provide a selection of books that students can check out and read on their own.

Explain that each American Indian group had its own religious beliefs. Some American Indian beliefs were tied to their daily routines. For example, it was common for groups to worship and give thanks to certain spirits before hunting and harvesting. *Spirit Animals: Meaning and Stories* by Wayne Arthurson is a text that may help students in their examination of American Indian beliefs.

As an alternative, ask the local library to set aside a collection of American Indian texts about American Indian beliefs so that students can visit and check out a book.

How Does Where I Live Influence My Local Government?

Partners ⟨20⟩ minutes

Materials: Classroom or Library Media Center resources

Explain to students that a good government guarantees that people are protected and are given the opportunity to live productive lives. A government must consider and address a variety of factors, including the natural environment. For example, California passes laws restricting water usage in areas prone to drought. Explain that state and local governments in other areas of the United States deal with different environmental issues, such as municipal snow removal in areas with significant annual snowfall.

Have partners brainstorm the specific needs of the people in their town, city, or region. Then have students look at their local government Web site to find examples of how these needs are addressed.

Read Aloud: American Indian Legends

Small Groups (20) **minutes**

Materials: Read Aloud pages

Explain to students that they will be reading aloud American Indian folk tales. Distribute the blackline master **American Indian Legends,** which is the text of a Read Aloud about several American Indian legends concerning nature. Have students pay special attention to the Director's Notes. Then organize the students into small groups. Allow each group the time to read over their assigned story, and have students determine how the reading will be divided among the group members. Work with each group as they read aloud the stories. If necessary, provide support for any vocabulary students may be unfamiliar with. Tell students they should read with accuracy, appropriate rate, and expression. During the reading, the rest of the group members should listen quietly and not interrupt. After the reading is complete, ask students to think about and discuss the similarities between each legend. Then ask students to talk about which legend was their favorite and why.

ELL Support for English Language Learners

Speaking: Tell students that a single idea may be conveyed in any number of ways. Have students practice condensing some of the ideas presented in the folk tales.

Entering: Write two sentences for students: *I like to read. I like to cook.* Read the sentences with students, and discuss ways to combine the sentences. (Possible answer: I like to read and cook.) Then have pairs of students create a compound sentence from folk tales in the Read Aloud Model. (Possible answer: Animals were the chiefs, **so** animals hunted people.)

Emerging: Tell students that they will create compound sentences using coordinate conjunctions (e.g., *and*, *but*, *so*). Have students work with a partner to create a compound sentence from the folk tales in the Read Aloud. Provide this example:

Long, long ago people were not the chiefs. They did not hunt animals. (Possible answer: Long, long ago people were not the chiefs, **so** they did not hunt animals.)

Developing: Review with students how to create compound sentences using coordinate conjunctions (e.g. *but, and, so*). Then have students create a compound sentence from the folk tales in the Read Aloud.

Expanding: Tell students that they will create complex sentences using subordinate conjunctions (e.g., *because, even though, so*). Then have students work with a partner to condense two clauses in the folk tales. Model with the following example:

There was once a three-legged rabbit. He made himself a fourth leg. (Possible answer: There was once a three-legged rabbit **so** he made himself a fourth leg.)

Bridging: Tell students that they will create complex sentences using subordinate conjunctions in a variety of ways (e.g. *because, even though, that*). Then have students work independently to create complex sentences from the following two clauses: *They dressed in clothes others threw away and ate what others would not, scraps and such. No one cared about them.* (Possible answer: They dressed in clothes others threw away and ate what others would not, scraps and such, **because** no one cared about them.)

The First Americans

11

Quick Activity Teacher Material

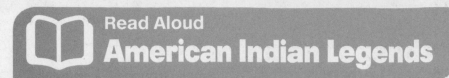

Director's Notes:

Read the following American Indian legends. Be careful to pace yourself and convey the tone of each sentence.

The Lost Children

Once upon a time, six young brothers became orphans. They dressed in old and cast-off clothing, and ate scraps and food that others would not touch. No one cared about them. They were loved only by a pack of dogs. They loved the dogs as much as the dogs loved them, and the brothers played with the dogs daily.

But people were unkind to them, because they wore ragged clothes and did not comb their hair. Other children, who wore fine buffalo robes, teased them. So the boys gave up on people. They did not want to be people any longer. They thought carefully about becoming flowers, but decided no, since the buffalo might eat them. They considered becoming stones, but decided no since stones could be broken. What about water? They wondered. But water could be drunk. Trees were lovely, but they could be slashed and burned.

They'd have to become stars. Stars are beautiful, of course, but they are also always and forever safe. The orphan brothers climbed the sky to become stars and were welcomed by the glorious Sun. The Moon loved them very much, too. In fact, she named them her lost children. Then, the Sun punished the unkind people below. She denied them water and created a drought. All the while the dogs howled at the sky, for they missed the boys. After some time the dog chief begged the Sun for pity. The dog chief explained that the drought hurt all creatures—not just the unkind. The Sun unleashed the rains.

Three-Legged Rabbit

There was once a three-legged rabbit, who made himself a fourth leg out of wood. Now the fact of the matter is that he thought that the Sun burned entirely too hot. He went to see just what could be done about it. He went to the east, right where the Sun would rise. And when the Sun rose halfway up, he shot it with an arrow, which made the Sun fall to the ground. As the Sun lay wounded, the three-legged rabbit got to work. To begin, he took the whites of the Sun's eyes and made plenty of clouds. He turned the black parts of the Sun's eyes to the sky. The kidneys he turned into stars, the liver into the Moon, and the heart into the night. "There!" exclaimed the three-legged rabbit. "The Sun will never be too hot again."

Little Brother Snares the Sun

Long, long ago people were not the chiefs. They did not hunt animals. Animals were the chiefs. Animals hunted people. They hunted people and killed them all, except a single girl and her little brother who hid from the animals in a cave. The boy learned the skill of killing snowbirds with a bow and arrow. From their feathers he made a robe. He and his sister made soup from what remained of the birds' bodies. This was when people first began to eat meat.

But the sunlight was too bright and eventually destroyed the boy's robe. The boy became filled with the desire for revenge. With his sister's help, he fashioned a snare. He took a trip to a hole in the ground. It was the hole from which the Sun rose every morning. Just as the Sun rose, the boy snared it. He tied it up, and there was no longer light or warmth for the day.

This feat both amazed and frightened the animals. So, they sent the most fearsome animal of all to free the Sun. The animal was a dormouse, which at the time was as big and as mighty as a mountain. The mouse did what she could. She used her great teeth to chew through the snare and free the Sun. But the intense heat shrunk her to her present size.

After that, people were the chiefs. They became the hunters, and the animals became the hunted.

Chapter 2

Age of Exploration

Objectives

- Describe the people and materials necessary for a successful sea voyage.
- Identify qualities and skills that would be helpful to a sea captain setting out on an uncertain journey.
- Recognize that choice and chance each play a role in the success of a risky venture.

Quest	**Project-Based Learning: Bon Voyage: A Seafaring Simulation**			
	Description	**Duration**	**Materials**	**Participants**
STEP 1 Set the Stage	Read a blackline master as an introduction to the project.	15 minutes	**Blackline Master:** Bon Voyage: A Seafaring Simulation	Whole Class
STEP 2 Launch the Activities		5 minutes	**Leveled Readers:** Preparing for a Voyage; Setting Sail: European Explorers; Ships to Shores: How the Early European Explorers Sailed to the Americas	Whole Class
Activity 1 Making a Budget	Make purchases for the voyage with a limited budget.	45 minutes	**Blackline Master:** Purchasing Supplies	Small Groups
Activity 2 Hiring Sailors ELL	Create a small poster as a recruiting tool.	25 minutes	**Materials:** Markers, scissors, glue/glue sticks, small sheets of posterboard	Small Groups
Activity 3 The Captain's Letters	Match short letters to their intended recipients.	20 minutes	**Blackline Master:** Letters from the Captain, prepared index cards	Small Groups
STEP 3 Complete the Quest A Seafaring Simulation	Complete the simulation using a gameboard.	20 minutes	**Blackline Master:** Anchors Aweigh!, game pieces (coins, counters, beans, or other pieces), six-sided dice	Small Groups
Answer the Compelling Question	Discuss the compelling question.	15 minutes		Whole Class

Quick Activities

	Description	Duration	Materials	Participants
Route Remembrance	Study, draw, and identify explorer routes.	15 minutes	**Blackline Master:** World Map or **Student Activity Mat** 5A The World, **Video:** Coronado National Memorial: Searching for Cities of Gold, classroom or Library Media Center resources	Partners
Primary Source: From *The Requerimiento* ELL	Read a primary source excerpt and write an essay response.	30 minutes	**Primary Source:** From *The Requerimiento*	Individual
Navigational Crossword Puzzle	Watch a short video and fill out crossword puzzle.	15 minutes	**Blackline Master:** Navigational Crossword, online access (optional)	Individual
Finding Coordinates	Use a GPS to find coordinates.	15 minutes	GPS software or Web site (such as Google Earth)	Small Groups
Readers Theater: Homeward Bound	Perform a brief skit about the reflections of Columbus and his crew on their journey home.	30 minutes	Script, props (optional)	Small Groups

Project-Based Learning: Bon Voyage: A Seafaring Simulation

How do people make decisions?

Welcome to Quest 2, Bon Voyage: A Seafaring Simulation. In this Quest, your students will participate in a simulation of a sea voyage across the Atlantic to the Americas. Through their study of what is required to make a voyage successful, they will be prepared to discuss the compelling question at the end of this inquiry.

Objectives

• Describe the people and materials necessary for a successful voyage.
• Identify qualities and skills that would be helpful to a sea captain setting out on an uncertain journey.
• Recognize that choice and chance each play a role in the success of a risky venture.

STEP 1 Set the Stage ⏱ 15 minutes

Begin the Quest by distributing the blackline master **Quest Kick Off,** It will bring the world of the Quest to life, introducing a story to interest students and a mission to motivate them.

Story

Students are sea captains and head crew in the European seaport of Explorania. Rumor has just reached their king and queen that land has been discovered by those sailing west across the Atlantic.

....

Mission

The royal family entrusts the students with a sum of money and instructs them to make the risky voyage across the sea and claim land for their kingdom.

STEP 2 Launch the Activities

The following three activities will help students prepare for their simulation by helping them make choices that will help to determine the outcome of their voyage. Note that all three can be done independently of the larger Quest. You may assign the appropriate Leveled Reader for this chapter.

Divide students into small groups that will remain consistent for all the activities.

Activity 1 Making a Budget (45) minutes

Materials: Blackline Master: Purchasing Supplies

Divide students into small groups, and explain that they have been given a sum of $4,500 by the royal family to make purchases for their voyage. They must make decisions: how many ships to buy, how many sailors to hire, and how much food to stock.

Distribute the blackline master **Purchasing Supplies,** which shows the kinds of supplies available to purchase and how much they cost.

Explain to the students that it is important to make the most of the funds that they are given, and they should take special care to make balanced choices in their purchases. Explain that the worksheet will be scored based on how well they have balanced the needs of the voyage, and that the higher their score, the higher their chances of successfully completing the voyage. Explain to students that they can use scratch paper to make calculations to help them with their decisions. See answer key for how to score the handouts.

Activity 2 **Hiring Sailors** (25) minutes

Materials: Markers, scissors, glue/glue sticks, small sheets of poster board

Students will create an illustrated poster to hang by the "docks" intended to attract the kind of sailor they are looking for. Discuss with the students beforehand the kind of qualities they would want in a crew that was going to make a long, uncertain voyage.

Encourage students to make careful decisions for word choice, noting that emphasizing certain aspects of the voyage will attract people with certain traits. After writing up a suitable "ad," students should choose or draw a picture intended to convey the same message as their written piece.

After each group has finished their ads, they can hang them on the board and take turns reading them out, and the class can offer feedback about the type of sailor they think each ad will attract. The posters will then be awarded between 1–5 points to be used at the end of the simulation. See answer key for grading scale.

ELL Support for English Language Learners

Speaking: Explain to students that when they offer opinions in a discussion, providing support for their opinions can help to persuade others. Remind students that they will need to offer their opinions in order to determine what to purchase during this activity.

Entering: Ask small groups to discuss their favorite color and then have each student explain why they like that color. Encourage students to express their opinion using the sentence form: *I think ____ is the best color because ____.*

Emerging: Hold up a pen for the students. Tell them that you think that if you drop the pen, it will fall on the desk. Ask the students whether they agree with you or disagree, and to provide one reason. Ask them for one reason why it might not fall on the desk (e.g., it might bounce and land on the floor). Have students write one opinion sentence in the form of *I think ... because ____.* Have the students share their sentences.

Developing: Offer students a hypothetical opinion about some item in the classroom (e.g., *I think that it would be better if those bookshelves were against the other wall*). Ask students whether they agree or disagree with the opinion. Encourage them to offer reasons for their agreement or disagreement.

Expanding: Have pairs of students discuss what they would like to do at recess. Encourage students to express their opinion with a sentence frame such as: *I would like to ____ because ____.* Remind students that adding more facts or details helps to strengthen their opinion. Then have each pair explain their ideas to the group.

Bridging: Place the students in pairs. Have one of the partners express an opinion (offer prompts if the students have difficulty thinking of a subject). Then have the other partner express the opposite opinion, and explain their reasoning. Then have the students switch roles. Emphasize the importance of being respectful and avoiding telling the other person that their opinion is bad, but rather trying to convince them by giving them reasons.

Activity 3 **The Captain's Letters** (20) **minutes**

Materials: Blackline Master: Letters from the Captain, prepared
index cards

Prepare five index cards with a name on one side and a short description on the
other in advance in the following manner:

Cartographer: I am a cartographer, which means I make maps.
I am useful to have on a journey because I will help
future sailors be able to plan their voyages well.

Patron: As a patron, I support the voyage with funds or supplies.

Navigator: A navigator such as myself keeps the ship on course by
determining her position based on measurements from
instruments such as a compass and a sextant.

Chief Steward: I, the Chief Steward, am responsible for making
sure our supplies and funds are used wisely.

First Mate: I am the captain's right-hand man. If anything were
to happen to the captain while we are on the voyage,
I would be the one to take command. I also help him
manage the crew.

Choose five volunteers, and hand each volunteer one of the prepared index cards.
Explain to the class that the captain has written letters to the people here who
are important to the voyage, but that he forgot to address them. The groups will
be responsible for delivering the letters to the correct people so as to finalize the
preparations for the voyage.

Distribute the blackline master **Letters from the Captain,** which shows the text of
five letters, and provides a space for writing in a name/title.

Have the volunteers read their cards out loud in front of the class. If desired,
write the names of the characters on the board. Then have the students read the
"letters" on their handout, and fill in the appropriate name/title for whom they
believe the letter to be written.

Groups' papers should be scored based on the number of correct answers,
0–5 points.

STEP 3 Complete the Quest

Part 1 Complete the Simulation ⏱ 20 minutes

Materials: Blackline Master: Anchors Aweigh!, game pieces (coins, counters, etc.), six-sided dice

Groups will be using the points that they have accrued over the course of the inquiry as the starting point for their voyage. Explain to the students that their points represent their level of preparedness for the voyage ahead; however, there is a degree of chance involved, and even the most prepared crews will not necessarily make it across the ocean.

Distribute the blackline master **Anchors Aweigh!** to each group, along with a game piece and a six-sided die. Explain to the students that they must move their game piece from the dock in Explorania to the shores of the new land, and that along the way, there are many things that can happen to their ships or their crew, and that each negative event will subtract from their point total. Students are only successful in the voyage if they make it to the shore without losing all of their points. Point out the "No Turning Back" line, and tell the students that if they run out of points before this line, they will be able to make it back to the mainland, but if they lose them after that point, then they will be considered lost at sea.

Have the students roll the die and move their game pieces along, deducting points as they move across, until they either successfully make it across the game board or lose their points along the way. Have students record whether the voyage was completed successfully, thus providing the outcome of the simulation. If time permits and if desired, allow the students to repeat the process several times to help them experience that both preparation and chance play a role in the success of a risky venture.

Part 2 Compelling Question ⏱ 15 minutes

After students complete the simulation, encourage them to reflect on what they learned. As a class, discuss the compelling question for this Quest "How do people make decisions?"

The students have learned the kinds of decisions and considerations necessary for a voyage akin to those the early European explorers made. Encourage students to consider the thought process that went into creating budgets and recruiting sailors. They should recall the degree to which chance played a role in the outcome, and consider how knowing the risks involved would impact their desire to commit to an uncertain venture. They should use what they learned to answer the compelling question.

BON VOYAGE:
A Seafaring Simulation

You are a sea captain in the European seaport of Explorania. Your king and queen have just told you that they have heard stories of explorers sailing west over the Atlantic Ocean and finding land. They don't want to fall behind—if others countries are going to claim land, they want to claim it too!

It's a risky voyage, and they cannot afford to spend too much. But they need someone trustworthy who will use the resources wisely, prepare well, and bravely take on the mission. Will the voyage be successful and reach the new lands? Or will the ships need to turn back—or worse, be lost at sea?

Your Mission

The royal family has entrusted you with the task of finding land over the sea and claiming it for Explorania! You will need to prepare well, and see if your preparations result in a successful voyage!

To help you prepare for your voyage, work with your team to do the following:

Activity 1   **Making a Budget:** Determine how to best spend your resources.

Activity 2   **Hiring Sailors:** Craft a "sailors wanted" poster to hire a good crew.

Activity 3   **The Captain's Letters:** Deliver short "letters" to their intended recipients to help the voyage start smoothly.

Complete Your Quest

Complete the simulation with the "points" you earn from each activity using the gameboard provided by your teacher.

Activity 1

Purchasing Supplies

Fill in the number of each type of supply you would like to purchase. Keep in mind the requirements! Points are deducted for ships that are not fully staffed and sailors that are not fully fed.

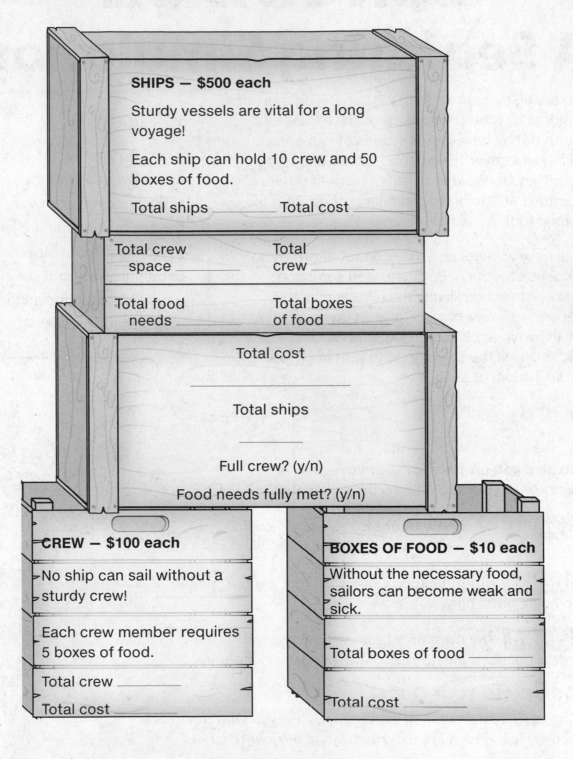

SHIPS — $500 each

Sturdy vessels are vital for a long voyage!

Each ship can hold 10 crew and 50 boxes of food.

Total ships _____   Total cost _____

Total crew space _____   Total crew _____

Total food needs _____   Total boxes of food _____

Total cost

_____

Total ships

_____

Full crew? (y/n)

Food needs fully met? (y/n)

CREW — $100 each

No ship can sail without a sturdy crew!

Each crew member requires 5 boxes of food.

Total crew _____

Total cost _____

BOXES OF FOOD — $10 each

Without the necessary food, sailors can become weak and sick.

Total boxes of food _____

Total cost _____

Letters from the Captain

Listen carefully to the descriptions read out loud. Then write the correct addressee in the blank space below each scroll to deliver the letters from the Captain.

Be sure you seal your traveling case well; seawater and maps do not mix!

_____

Procure, if you would, a good lock for the food stocks. I will have no thieves on my ship, and I know you feel the same.

_____

Let me again impress upon you how honored I am that you would be so gracious to provide us with such a sum! We will bring glory to Explorania.

_____

Are you sure your instruments are calibrated, or adjusted, correctly? The last thing we need is to end up lost.

Inform the crew that we board at dawn. And make sure they are on board early. Anyone late will peel onions for a month.

Quest Findings

Anchors Aweigh!

Using the points you collected during the Quest, move your piece along the gameboard, subtracting from your total as directed. If you run out of points before the "No Turning Back" line, you head back to shore. If you run out of points after the line, you are lost at sea. If you make it to the end without losing all of your points, congratulations! Your crew made it successfully to land!

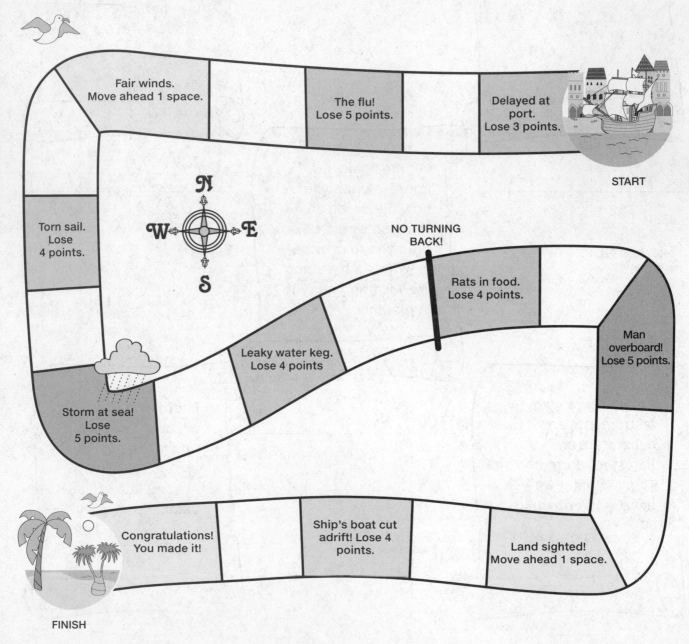

Fair winds. Move ahead 1 space.

The flu! Lose 5 points.

Delayed at port. Lose 3 points.

START

Torn sail. Lose 4 points.

NO TURNING BACK!

Rats in food. Lose 4 points.

Man overboard! Lose 5 points.

Leaky water keg. Lose 4 points

Storm at sea! Lose 5 points.

Congratulations! You made it!

Ship's boat cut adrift! Lose 4 points.

Land sighted! Move ahead 1 space.

FINISH

Quick Activities

Route Remembrance

Partners 15 minutes

Materials: Blackline Master: World Map or **Student Activity Mat** 5A The World, Video: Coronado National Memorial: Searching for Cities of Gold (optional), classroom or Library Media Center resources

Divide students into pairs, and instruct them to research the routes of the following explorers: Cortés, de Soto, Coronado, Magellan.

Distribute the blackline master **World Map** or **Student Activity Mat** 5A The World, which is a blank world map.

Once both students have found the routes of each explorer, have each student draw the route of one of the explorers from memory without telling his/her partner which explorer they are drawing. Students will then exchange papers and try to guess the explorer whose route each was charting.

If desired and if time permits, have students watch the video about Coronado National Memorial Park.

Primary Source: From *The Requerimiento*

Individual (30) minutes

Materials: Primary Source: From *The Requerimiento*

Explain to the students that they will be reading an excerpt from a text called *The Requerimiento*. Note that the word "requerimiento" is the Spanish word for "request," or "demand," and that this document was a declaration meant to be read to American Indians encountered by Spanish explorers asserting that American Indians had an obligation to accept the sovereignty of both the Catholic Church and the Spanish monarchy.

Distribute the blackline master **Primary Source: From *The Requerimiento*** which shows an excerpt from the above-named document.

After the students read the handout, write the following question on the board:

How do you think the Spanish monarchy viewed the American Indian people to whom they were writing?

Have students write a short essay response to the question, citing three examples from the text.

(ELL) Support for English Language Learners

Writing: Remind students that word choice affects how descriptive sentences sound. Explain that color and nuance can be added to a sentence by adding descriptive language, such as adjectives, or adding embedded clauses. (e.g., *The excited dog jumped* vs. *The frightened dog jumped*) or an embedded clause (e.g., *The dog, who had an injured leg, jumped*.)

Entering: Provide students with basic sentences, such as *It is sunny. I like carrots.* Review with students the role of adjectives and adverbs in sentences. Ask pairs to write two basic sentences. Have pairs switch sentences and have each pair write more interesting sentences.

Emerging: Place the students in pairs. Have each student write a simple sentence. Then have students switch sentences and ask each student to rewrite his/her partner's sentence, but with an adjective that adds more description.

Developing: Review with students that their essays will be more interesting if they include adjectives and adverbs to their writing. To help students write more interesting sentences, suggest they think of *wh-* questions, such as *where, when, why, how*.

Expanding: Provide the sentence *The frog hopped onto a stone*. Ask the students to expand on the sentence by adding an embedded clause. Have volunteers read their sentences to the class.

Bridging: Review the concept of an embedded clause with the students, and remind them that adjectives describe nouns. Have each student write a simple subject-verb-object sentence. Then have the students rewrite their sentences using adjectives and embedded clauses.

Navigational Crossword Puzzle

Materials: Blackline Master: Navigational Crossword, online access (optional)

If desired, download the video *The Longitude Problem* (http://mpbn. pbslearningmedia.org/resource/segment-longitude-timeandnavigation-stemin30/the-longitude-problem-stem-in-30), or stream it directly to students. Have students watch the video to give them background information about the problem with determining longitude before modern instruments.

Distribute the blackline master **Navigational Crossword,** which is a crossword puzzle using navigational terms.

Explain to the students that the invention of the chronometer by John Harrison in 1735 allowed ships to keep track of time accurately while at sea, since mechanical clocks were affected by the motion of a ship. Navigational instruments such as the astrolabe and the sextant used the position of the ship in relation to the stars, the sun, or (in the case of the sextant), the moon to chart the course of a ship. Explain the function of the equator and the prime meridian, especially in relation to determining longitude and latitude. Then have the students complete the crossword puzzle.

Finding Coordinates

Materials: GPS software or Web site (such as Google Earth)

Students will use Global Positioning System (GPS) software or Web sites (such as Google Earth) to determine the coordinates of several important locations.

Review the concept of coordinates with the class, and provide examples of how coordinates are written. Explain that GPS technology is a modern way to find one's position on the globe, which is what the European explorers were using their navigational tools for. Explain that GPS is a form of satellite technology that can tell a user the geographic coordinates of a physical address. Then instruct students to use the GPS technology to look up coordinates for the following locations, and explain the significance of each:

- Genoa, Italy (Columbus' hometown)

- Bahamas (Where Columbus is believed to have first landed; have students look up the modern capital, Nassau)

- the White House, Washington, D.C. (U.S. Capital)

- your school's coordinates

- Orcadas Antarctic Base (the first permanent research base in Antarctica; point out to students that this is an example of how the past tradition of global exploration continues to the present day)

World Map

Draw the route of your chosen explorer on the map. Then trade papers with a partner and guess each other's chosen explorers.

From *The Requerimiento*

Read this excerpt from *The Requerimiento*. *The Requerimiento* was a document that Spanish explorers read to American Indians. As you read it, use the vocabulary section to help with difficult words.

Vocabulary

obliged, *v.,* required

charity, *n.,* benevolent goodwill

servitude, *n.,* the condition of having to obey someone else

compel, *v.,* force

"If you do so, you will do well, and that which you are **obliged** to do to their Highnesses, and we in their name shall receive you in all love and **charity**, and shall leave you, your wives, and your children, and your lands, free without **servitude**, that you may do with them and with yourselves freely that which you like and think best, and they shall not **compel** you to turn Christians . . .

But, if you do not do this ... with the help of God, we shall powerfully enter into your country, and shall make war against you in all ways and manners that we can ... we shall take you and your wives and your children, and shall make slaves of them ... and we shall take away your goods, and shall do you all the mischief and damage that we can ..."

Navigational Crossword Puzzle

Fill in the crossword puzzle with the vocabulary words using the clues provided.

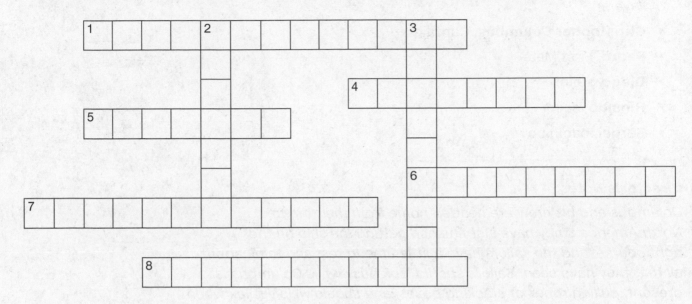

ACROSS

1. _____ the Imaginary line designated as being the starting point for measurement of longitude, or 0 degrees

4. _____ the measurement of position based on distance north or south of the equator

5. _____ a more accurate tool for determining latitude than the astrolabe

6. _____ the measurement of position based on distance east or west of the prime meridian; measurement requires accurate timekeeping

7. _____ the name of the inventor credited with inventing the first accurate chronometer

8. _____ an instrument invented in the 18th century that allowed navigators to keep time accurately while at sea despite the movements of the ship

DOWN

2. _____ the imaginary line dividing Earth into northern and southern hemispheres

3. _____ an instrument used to help calculate latitude before the invention of the sextant

VOCABULARY:
astrolabe
chronometer
prime meridian
equator
latitude
John Harrison
sextant
longitude

A story about how Columbus and his sailors may have discussed their first journey to the Americas.

The Parts

5 players:

- **Christopher Columbus**, Captain
- **Pedro**, First Mate
- **Diego**, sailor
- **Rinaldo**, sailor
- **Sergei**, cabin boy

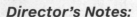

Director's Notes:

Columbus and his crew are headed home from their trip to North America. They have just finished getting the ship on the right course, and the sailors have a little time to rest and think about all that they have seen. Sailors should look busy while Columbus is present, pulling ropes or stacking boxes, and should visibly relax when he leaves the stage.

Pedro:	We've a good wind, Captain. I think we're starting our journey home on the right foot now.
Columbus:	The right foot cannot begin to describe ... Pedro, I have done it! I have found the Indies! Think what this means for Spain! A trade route by sea! The things to come, the spices, the trade ... all without the interference of merchants who increase the prices for their goods each time they change hands (which I think they aim to do as many times as they can!). Furthermore, we can send missionaries there. Pedro! I can imagine how happy that will make Queen Isabella. And the island that the Indians spoke of, the one they say is filled with gold.
Pedro:	Their Majesties will likely be happy to hear that as well!

| **Columbus:** | Indeed, I am sure that they will be happy with all our report. But for now, I will retire below deck. I intend to write a letter to their Majesties while on board, and I believe that I will begin it. |

Captain Columbus exits the stage.

| **Diego:**
raising his eyebrows | Well, the Captain is in good spirits. |

| **Rinaldo:** | Aye, and who can blame him? Are there any that can deny his report now? We've seen it, we've seen the Indies with our own eyes, just like he said we would! |

| **Diego:**
shrugging slightly | I'm glad to be headed home, to tell you the truth. |

| **Rinaldo:**
chuckling | Had a bit too much adventure, have you? |

| **Diego:**
thoughtfully | I don't know if you'd call it that … I'm as all in for adventure and glory and riches as the next sailor. I'm just trying to wrap my head around what we saw. People! We saw people. And we talked to them, and ate with them … |

| **Pedro:** | I won't deny, my heart just about jumped into my throat when I saw them there. |

| **Rinaldo:**
pointing at him | And you weren't the only one, not by a long shot. |

| **Sergei:**
remembering, with wide eyes | The people there looked as scared as we felt. |

| **Pedro:** | Well, they thought the ship was some kind of heavenly creature or thing, didn't they? |

| **Rinaldo:** | Something like that. We were lucky that they were friendly. |

Pedro:

They really were, weren't they? Hardly a weapon in sight, only spears, and it seemed like they were ready to trade anything!

Diego:
gesturing towards Rinaldo

And *for* anything. You were trying to trade them some broken bits of pottery, weren't you?

Rinaldo:
shrugging sheepishly and apologetically

Maybe a few ... but the Captain stopped me. Said it wasn't right.

Diego:

I don't always agree with him, but I do this time. He gave them things too, without trading anything for them. Bolts of cloth, and whatnot. He said the Queen would want him to be friendly and generous.

Rinaldo:

He's no fool, I guess. I suppose this proves it.

Diego:

Still. Where are all the spices? We're bringing plants, and especially that plant that the Indians were smoking—what did they call it?

Pedro:

Tobacco, I think ...?

Diego:

That's it, yes ... and some gold; jewelry and whatnot. I just find it odd that we wouldn't find anything of the kind we were looking for.

Sergei:
dreamily

I will always remember how beautiful it was. I've never seen trees like that. I don't think there are trees like that anywhere in Europe, or maybe anywhere else in the whole world!

Pedro:
fondly smiling at Sergei

The world's a large place, Sergei. Larger than perhaps any of us know. I know one thing for sure, though. I'll be thinking about this voyage for a long, long time.

Settling the Colonies in North America

Objectives

- Identify the political borders of the European colonies in North America.
- Describe the particular attributes of the individual colonies.
- Demonstrate knowledge of the advantages and hardships of colonial life in North America.

Quest Project-Based Learning: Colonial Open House

	Description	Duration	Materials	Participants
STEP 1 Set the Stage	Read a blackline master as an introduction to the project.	15 minutes	**Blackline Master:** Quest Kick Off	Whole Class
STEP 2 Launch the Activities	Divide students into small groups and assign colonies.	5 minutes	**Leveled Readers:** The Colonies of North America; Europe's Colonies in North America; Europe in North America: A History of the Colonies	Small Groups
Activity 1 Mapping Your Territory	Draw the borders of the assigned colony.	20 minutes	**Blackline Master:** Brochure Cover!, **Student Activity Mat:** 1A United States, markers, crayons, colored pencils	Small Groups
Activity 2 Identifying Motivations	Discover reasons for immigration to the colonies.	25 minutes	Large index cards, classroom or Library Media Center resources	Small Groups
Activity 3 Illustrating Your Brochure	Create artwork for the brochure.	20 minutes	Colored pencils, crayons or markers; brochures for local attractions (optional)	Small Groups
Activity 4 Interviewing Colonists	Simulate two interviews and select quotes.	30 minutes	**Blackline Master:** Interviewing Colonists	Small Groups
STEP 3 ELL Complete the Quest Assemble the Brochures	Write text for and assemble brochures.	45 minutes	Completed Quest materials, various art supplies (optional), scissors, glue or glue sticks, binder clips, paper clips, or staplers	Small Groups
Hold the Open House	Host a Colonial Open House.	45 minutes		Small Groups
Answer the **Compelling Question**	Discuss the compelling question.	15 minutes		Whole Class

Quick Activities

	Description	Duration	Materials	Participants
Primary Source: "The New Colossus"	Analyze an excerpt from the poem "The New Colossus ."	(15) minutes	**Primary Source:** The New Colossus	Individual
Colonial Comparisons	Complete a chart comparing Jamestown and Plymouth.	(25) minutes	**Blackline Master:** Comparing Jamestown and Plymouth	Partners
A Day in the Life ELL	Create a to-do list for a fictional colonist.	(20) minutes	Classroom or Library Media Center resources	Small Groups
Which Religion Would Your Colony Be?	Create a spinner and discuss colonial religious traditions.	(30) minutes	**Blackline Master:** Create a Spinner, scissors, cardboard or cardstock, glue or glue sticks, brass round-head fasteners, tape, paper clips, binder clips, or staplers	Small Groups
Readers Theater: Decisions in Jamestown	Perform a brief skit about the colonists' decision to stay in Jamestown.	(30) minutes	Script, props, such as hats or clothing (optional)	Small Groups

Project-Based Learning: Colonial Open House

Q^{Compelling}**uestion** ## Why did some people in Europe decide to move to colonies in North America?

Welcome to Quest 3, Colonial Open House. In this Quest, your students will be acting as travel agents of the Spanish, Virginian, Massachusetts, French, and Dutch colonies, creating brochures and staging an Open House for prospective immigrants to the North American colonies. Through their study of the attributes of their assigned colonies, they will be prepared to discuss the compelling question at the end of this inquiry.

Objectives

- Identify the political borders of the European colonies in North America.
- Describe the particular attributes of the individual colonies.
- Demonstrate knowledge of the advantages and hardships of colonial life in North America.

STEP 1 Set the Stage 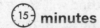 minutes

Begin the Quest by distributing the blackline master **Quest Kick Off**. It will bring the world of the Quest to life, introducing a story to interest students and a mission to motivate them.

Story

Disaffected Europeans in the early 1600s have decided to attend an Open House in order to explore their options for emigration. The Europeans of each nation want information on the various colonies of North America.

....

Mission

Students have been selected by their colony's representatives to act as travel agents at the Open House. Their mission is to prepare a brochure for the Europeans in attendance in an attempt to convince them to move to the colony the students represent.

STEP 2 Launch the Activities

The following four activities will help students prepare for the creation of their brochure by researching their assigned colonies and gathering information. Note that all four can be done independently of the larger Quest. You may assign the appropriate Leveled Reader for this chapter.

Divide students into small groups that will remain consistent for all the activities. Each small group should be assigned one of the following:

- Spanish colonies
- Virginian colonies
- Massachusetts colonies
- French colonies
- Dutch colonies

Activity 1 Mapping Your Territory ⓴ minutes

Materials: Student Activity Mat: 1A United States, Blackline Master
Brochure Cover!, markers, crayons, colored pencils

Students will be drawing the political borders of their assigned territories as the cover page for their brochure.

Distribute the blackline master **Brochure Cover!,** which shows a blank map of North America with a space for a title at the top and will serve as the title page for the brochure. Alternatively, you may want to have students look at the Student Activity Mat and discuss the area that made up the original colonies that they are writing about.

Direct the students to use print and/or Internet resources, such as the Web site https://www.learner.org/interactives/historymap/colonists.html, where they can look up the borders of their territories in the early 1600s. Students should draw and color in the borders of their assigned territories in an attractive way meant to draw the eye of a potential immigrant. Explain to the students that this will be the cover of their brochure. Encourage students to note the size differences among the colonies as they research, and explain that not all European countries were represented equally in North America. Point out the line for a title at the top of the handout, and instruct students that although they may label their territories (or rivers, landmarks, etc.) on the map portion itself, that they should leave the title blank for the time being. Titles for their brochures will be added as one of the final steps of completing the inquiry.

Activity 2 Identifying Motivations minutes

Materials: Large index cards, classroom or Library Media Center resources

Explain to students that they will be looking at reasons that Europeans had for moving to the colonies in North America. Be sure that students understand that in this activity, they will be researching the conditions in Europe in the early 1600s for the countries that own their colonies (e.g., the group representing the Dutch colonies will research the Netherlands, the group representing the Virginia colonies will research England, etc.). Give each group a large index card. Then write the following questions on the board:

• Why did your country first set up a colony in the Americas?

• Does your country have any persecuted religious groups? If so, who?

• Are there many opportunities for poor people to become successful in your home country?

Students should conduct research using print and/or Internet-based materials in order to find the answers to these questions, and they should write the answers on their index cards using complete sentences. The following URLs may be helpful:

• http://www.granburyisd.org/cms/lib/TX01000552/Centricity/ Domain/287/Fact_Sheet_U1_Comparison_of_Eng_Fr_Sp_Col.pdf

• http://history-world.org/united_states_of_america.htm (search for the country name under the heading "COLONIAL EXPERIMENTS")

Once students have found the answers to these questions, the groups should take turns presenting their information to the class. When the groups have completed their presentations, review with the students the idea that economic betterment and desire for religious freedom were among the more universal reasons that people had for coming to the colonies. Explain that the colonies differed in how they addressed these concerns (e.g., Spanish colonists were interested in finding gold, French colonists were interested in trading with Indians for valuable furs, British colonists were interested in agriculture).

Encourage students to recognize that knowing the reasons that Europeans had for seeking a new life in the colonies will help them to design their brochures to appeal to the concerns of these prospective colonists.

Activity 3 | Illustrating Your Brochure (20) minutes

Materials: Colored pencils, crayons or markers; brochures for local
attractions (optional)

Explain to the students that they will be creating several pieces of artwork for their
brochures. Students should conduct print and/or Internet research to determine
the qualities of each colony, and produce artwork based on what qualities they
would like to emphasize. Remind students that a brochure is designed to attract
attention and interest, and emphasize that the pictures that they draw are
essential elements of creating a convincing brochure. If desired, have students
pass around brochures for local attractions for reference, and point out specific
examples of how the artwork contributes to the overall effect. Encourage students
to caption their work.

Remind the students that the artwork should address the concerns of the people
of Europe (as determined in the previous activity). For example, if their colony
offers freedom from religious persecution, an effective piece of artwork might
consist of a church filled with happily praying people, accompanied by the caption
"Freedom to worship as you choose!" Be sure that students understand that
they can appeal to religious freedom, the promise of land ownership, and a good
growing climate among other reasons, and that they are making stylistic decisions
about what to emphasize in their brochures (e.g., adventure, stability, prosperity).

Students within the small groups should be encouraged to confer with one
another to plan the artwork and maximize the variety of imagery.

Activity 4 Interviewing Colonists ⏱ 30 minutes

Materials: Blackline Master: Interviewing Colonists

Students will be simulating an "interview" of two fictional residents of their colonies, one male and one female. The students will, using print and/or Internet materials, research the living conditions of those living in their assigned colonies during the late 16ᵗʰ and early 17ᵗʰ centuries, and formulate their answers according to the information they find. The students will then name their fictional colonists.

Distribute two copies of the blackline master **Interviewing Colonists** which provides a list of questions that the students will use in their simulated interviews.

Explain to the students that they should imagine themselves in the roles of their fictional colonists and answer the interview questions in the person of their imagined interviewees. Once they have done this, students can choose two quotes from the interviews that they think would be most helpful for including in their brochures. Remind students to choose quotes in keeping with the overall sense of what they want to convey in their brochures. Students should put a star next to the quotes that they choose.

STEP 3 Complete the

Part 1 Assemble the Brochures ⏱ 45 minutes

Materials: Completed Quest materials, various art supplies (optional), scissors, glue or glue sticks, binder clips, paper clips, or staplers

Using the research that they completed and resources that they created during the inquiry, students will write the main text for and complete their brochures. Encourage students to incorporate their artwork and their quotes in such a way as to maximize visual interest, and to frame the text of their brochures to support the overall sense of their assigned colonies that they want to convey. Allow the students to title their brochures, encouraging them to come up with a creative title based on what they have discovered about their colonies during the course of the inquiry. Though the length of the brochure will vary somewhat based on student selections/preferences, the brochures should be at least three pages (no more than six), contain at least three pictures, two quotes, and enough main text to thoroughly inform a reader. Students can add decorative elements to their brochures as time allows.

Support for English Language Learners

Writing: Explain to students that certain kinds of writing require putting a lot of information into a small space, and that one way to condense their writing is to combine several clauses, or verb-noun combinations, into one sentence.

Entering: Write these sentences on the board, and then read them to students: *The Southern colonies are warmer. The Southern colonies grow many crops.* Discuss with students how they might condense these sentences to make them quicker to read. (Possible answer: *The Southern colonies are warmer and grow many crops.*) Repeat with other sentence pairs.

Emerging: Write these sentences on the board: *The colonists lived in Massachusetts.* and *The colonists were looking for religious freedom.* Ask students how the sentences can be combined. With student input, combine the information in the two sentences into one, and write the new sentence on the board (e.g., *The colonists who were looking for religious freedom lived in Massachusetts*). Write two more example sentences on the board for them to combine.

Developing: On the board, write out the sentences *The colonists wanted religious freedom. The colonists were Puritans.* and *The colonists lived in Plymouth.* Explain that these sentences can be combined into a single sentence, such as *The Puritan colonists who wanted religious freedom lived in Plymouth.* Explain that the single sentence offers more information in a shorter space than the multiple sentences, and reads more smoothly in English. Then write one single-clause sentence on the board describing something (e.g., *Many Europeans were poor.* or *There was land in North America.*). Have each student write an additional sentence about the subject (e.g., *Many Europeans were unhappy.* and *Many Europeans decided to move to the colonies.*) Then have the students work together to combine their clauses into a single sentence.

Expanding: Have students work in pairs or small groups. On the board write several sentences: *Dutch families settled in New Amsterdam. People traded furs, timber, and tobacco. People from many countries came to New Amsterdam.* Ask each group to write new sentences. (Possible answer: *People from many countries came to New Amsterdam to trade furs, timber, and tobacco.*) Explain to students that when you combine sentences, you do not have to use all the words from the original sentences. Your goal is to convey the same information and make your sentence readable and interesting. Provide several more sentences for students and have groups work together to create more concise and interesting sentences.

Bridging: Write these sentences: *The colonists were determined. There were many hardships in the colonies.* and *The colonists overcame many hardships because they were so determined.* Explain to students that they can combine these sentences to make a single, more complex sentence that reads more smoothly in English and conveys more information in a smaller space. Have students suggest how the sentences might combine into a single sentence. (Possible answers: *The determination of the colonists allowed them to overcome the many hardships.* or *The many hardships were overcome by the colonists' determination.*) In small groups, have the students write three sentences with separate, but related, clauses. Then have students combine the sentences to form a single, multiple-clause sentence.

Hold the Open House ⏲ **minutes**

Allow each group to set up a "station" somewhere in the classroom where they can display their brochures. If possible, invite community members, faculty members, or another class to the Open House. Alternatively, divide the class into two groups, allowing half of the class to represent their groups while the other half browses the Open House, and then switching. If other students, faculty or community members are present, provide some background material or presentation concerning the nature of the students' inquiry (you may wish to pass out the **Quest Kick Off** handout to the visitors for this purpose).

Participants should then walk around and browse the brochures of the different groups (if completing the activity as a class, be sure to allow enough time for each half of the class to be able to adequately view the other groups' brochures). Students representing their groups should be standing with their brochure and be available to answer questions from the participants.

If desired and if time permits, when participants have finished browsing, you can lead a discussion asking participants which colonies they are most drawn to and why based on the information gleaned from the activity.

 Compelling Question ⏲ **minutes**

After students have hosted the Open House, encourage them to reflect on what they learned. As a class, discuss the compelling question for this Quest: "Why did some people in Europe decide to move to colonies in North America?"

Students have learned about the attributes of the various European colonies in North America. Encourage them to think about the appeal that these colonies had for people in Europe. They should use what they learned to answer the compelling question.

Colonial Open House

Rumors have reached the shores of Europe that the North American colonies offer new opportunities. Many people from Europe have decided to attend a Colonial Open House to find out more. Representatives from each of the North American colonies will attend and provide information about their colonies.

Your colony's representatives have chosen you to act as travel agents to attend the Open House and attract new colonists.

Your Mission

As travel agents, your job is to represent your colony. It is up to you to create an attractive brochure and a presentation to persuade Europeans who might want to move that your colony is the one for them!

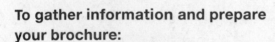

To gather information and prepare your brochure:

Activity 1 **Mapping Your Territory**: Draw in the borders of your colony.

Activity 2 **Identifying Motivations**: Determine some of the reasons that Europeans had for immigrating.

Activity 3 **Illustrating Your Brochure:** Create artwork representative of life in your colony.

Activity 4 **Interviewing Colonists:** Simulate an interview of two colonists to gather quotes.

Complete Your Quest

Attend the Colonial Open House, displaying your brochure and discussing your colony with the attendees.

Activity 1

Brochure Cover!

Draw and color in the borders of your territory. Label nearby lakes, rivers, or landmarks. Finally, title your brochure on the line provided.

_____

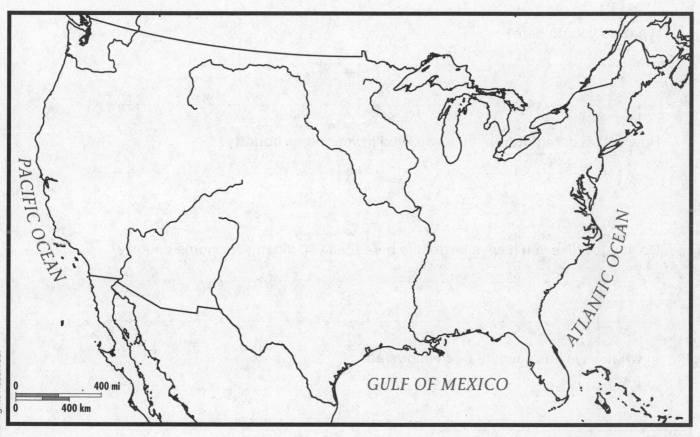

Interviewing Colonists

Imagine yourselves in the role of a colonist in your assigned territory.
Complete the interview questions as if you were this colonist.

Colonist's Name _____

Why did you come to this colony?

_____

_____

What do you do here?

_____

_____

How is this different from how you lived in your home country?

_____

_____

Do you feel like you have a better life here than you did in your home country?

_____

_____

In what ways has your life been improved?

_____

_____

Quick Activities

Primary Source: "The New Colossus" Individual (15) minutes

Materials: Primary Source: The New Colossus

Distribute the blackline master **Primary Source: The New Colossus,** which shows an excerpt from Emma Lazarus' poem "The New Colossus."

Explain to the students that this is an excerpt from a poem about the Statue of Liberty. The statue came to be symbolic for the idea that the United States is a "land of opportunity." The students should read the text to themselves, and answer the question at the bottom of the page. Remind students that vocabulary words are bolded in the text and defined.

Then lead a class discussion about how the "American Dream" has its basis in the early colonists and their hopes for a better life, and has continued to be a fundamental part of the American ethos to the present day. Point out that while the sentiments may sound familiar to the students from their studies of the early colonies, the poem was written in 1883, more than 200 years after the first colonists began arriving in North America. If desired, discuss the significance of Ellis Island and its relationship to European immigration, as well as the significance of Angel Island and its relationship to Asian immigration in California.

Colonial Comparisons

Partners (25) **minutes**

Materials: Blackline Master: Comparing Jamestown and Plymouth

Students will conduct research using print and/or Internet materials to complete a chart comparing the settlements at Jamestown and Plymouth:

- Government

- Economy

- Religion

- Social structure

- Geography/Climate

Web sites such as the following can be used as part of the students' research:

https://www.nps.gov/jame/learn/historyculture/jamestown-and-plymouth-compare-and-contrast.htm

Distribute the blackline master **Comparing Jamestown and Plymouth**, which gives students a chart for the settlements at Jamestown and Plymouth.

Once the chart is filled out, direct the pairs of students to take turns asking one another the question; *Which colony would you have preferred to live in, and why?* Students should explain their answers based on the research that they have conducted.

A Day in the Life

Materials: Classroom or Library Media Center resources

Students will create a "to-do list" for a fictional character of their choice from the colonial times. Students will choose a representative "character" from the colonies (e.g., a New England farm wife; a Pennsylvania Quaker, a Virginia boy on a plantation) and conduct research to create a day plan for their character. Instruct students to include information such as what time they will wake up, the kind of food they plan to eat, the kinds of tasks they will engage in, the kinds of recreation they will participate in, and the time they will go to sleep. Students should make at least seven entries, and may illustrate their day plan if they choose.

The following resources can be made available to students:

- http://www.historyisfun.org/pdf/colonial-life/Colonial_Life.pdf

- *If You Lived in Colonial Times* by Ann McGovern

ELL Support for English Language Learners

Speaking and Listening: Explain to students that when writing in small groups, it is important to be able to appropriately express ideas for the group to consider.

Entering: Ask students to tell you a favorite after-school activity. Then have groups discuss an activity that the group might want to do. Encourage each member of the group to share an idea. Suggest they use the phrase *I think ...* to share their idea.

Emerging: Divide the students into small groups. Propose a situation where the students are on a school committee trying to plan a class party. Have each student in the group take turns making a suggestion for a food that could be served at the party, using the phrase *I think ...* to express their opinions.

Developing: Review with students how to work in a group, take turns speaking, listen to each other, and offer useful comments. Divide students into small groups. Propose to students a situation where they are on a school committee trying to plan a school activity to take place on the weekend. Have each student in the group suggest an activity and explain why it would be fun. Suggest they use the sentence frame: *I think we should ____ because ____.*

Expanding: Have pairs of students pretend to plan a class party. Have one student in each pair suggest an activity that the class could do at the party. After each suggestion, the partner should comment on the suggestion, stating whether they think that the suggestion is a good idea or not, and why/why not.

Bridging: Have small groups of students imagine they are on a school committee trying to plan a class party. Have each student offer an opinion on an activity that the class can do at the party, offering reasons why they think that the activity is appropriate. After each suggestion, the group should take turns offering reasons why they agree or disagree with the original speaker, and offering ideas on how to improve it.

Which Religion Would Your Colony Be? Small Groups minutes

Materials: Blackline Master: Create a Spinner, scissors, cardboard or
cardstock, glue or glue sticks, brass round-head fasteners,
tape, paperclips, binder clips, or staplers

Students will create a spinner using the handout, which they will then
use to determine which colony they are "from" for the purposes of the
exercise.

Distribute the blackline master **Create a Spinner,** which gives directions
on how to create a spinner.

Students will first assemble and then take turns spinning the spinner,
which is divided into four sections (Virginia, New England, Pennsylvania,
Maryland). Once students have all taken turns with the spinner, tally
results from each group, and write the results on the board. Then explain
that the different colonies largely followed different religious traditions.

Explain that the students in Virginia would be Anglicans, who are
followers of the Church of England. Those in Maryland would be
Catholics, who follow the teachings of the Pope. Pennsylvanian students
would be Quakers, a pacifist Christian religion emphasizing the direct
relationship between God and believers. Finally, the New Englanders
would be Puritans, a group seeking to "purify" the Church of England of
its perceived excesses. Point out that in many cases, religious principles
were encoded in the laws of the colonies, and that in some cases church
attendance was compulsory. Also review the concept of freedom of
religion, and note to the students that it is notably absent in many of the
colonies (as well as in many European countries) during this time period,
and was a later development in American politics.

The New Colossus

Both Ellis Island and Angel Island were immigration inspection stations that operated in the late nineteenth to early twentieth centuries. The Statue of Liberty is located near Ellis Island, and the following excerpt is from a poem which is inscribed on a plaque at the base of the statue. Read the passage. Then answer the question below.

Statue of Liberty

"Give me your tired, your poor,

Your **huddled** masses **yearning** to breathe free,

The **wretched refuse** of your **teeming** shore.

Send these, the homeless, **tempest**-tossed to me,

I lift my lamp beside the golden door!"

– from "The New Colossus," Emma Lazarus

Statue of Liberty

Vocabulary

huddled, *adj.,* crowded together

yearning, *v.,* longing

wretched, *adj.,* unfortunate, miserable

refuse, *n.,* cast-away(s)

teeming, *adj.,* full

tempest, *n.,* storm

Angel Island

1. What do you think the passage means by, "I lift my lamp beside the golden door "?

_____

_____

Name _____ Date _____

Comparing Jamestown and Plymouth

As you conduct research on the colonies, fill in the chart below with information about Jamestown and Plymouth.

	Jamestown	Plymouth
Government		
Economy		
Religion		
Social structure (types of settlers, role of women, etc.)		
Geography/Climate		

Create a Spinner

Make and spin this spinner—whatever it lands on is the colony you're from!

You'll Need:
Scissors, cardboard or cardstock, glue or glue sticks, 1 brass round-head fastener, tape, 1 paper clip

1. Cut out your circle and glue it to a piece of cardboard or cardstock.

2. Push a brass fastener through the middle of the circle (you can use a pencil or pen to start the hole) so that part of it is sticking up (should not be flat against the spinner on the top) and fold the edges underneath. Secure folded edges flat against the back of the spinner with tape.

3. Place a paper clip over the fastener so that it can rotate freely.

4. Use your spinner!

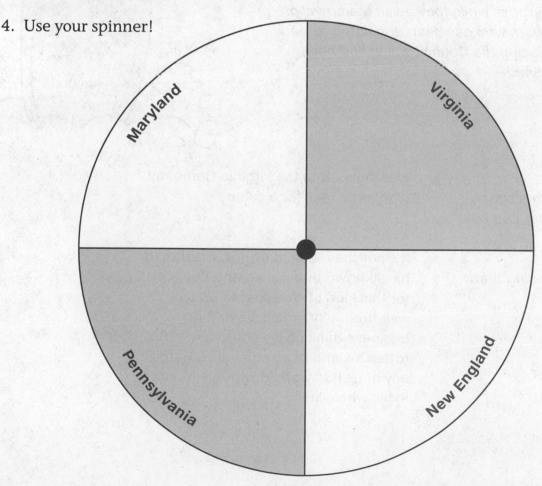

A story about the first colonists at Jamestown, and their decision to stay.

The Parts

5 players:

- **Robert Ford,** gentleman colonist
- **Thomas Sands,** gentleman colonist
- **William Johnson,** laborer
- **Nicholas Houlgrave,** gentleman colonist
- **Baron De La Warr,** appointed governor of Virginia

Director's Notes:

Settlers from Jamestown are sitting aboard one of the ships that they intend to sail to England. Dejected, they intend to give up on their settlement due to hardships. They discuss the reasons for the apparent failure of their colonial enterprise while they await the arrival of Governor De La Warr, who has been appointed to lead the colonies, replacing the Council which had been headed by John Smith.

Robert:
sarcastically, with disgust, making an exaggerated bow

Well, hats off to the Virginia Company. Wonderful idea for a colony.

Thomas:
looking and sounding tired

It's not their fault, it's ours; we should have known that we weren't cut out for this kind of life. Most of us are well-bred gentlemen; we had no business thinking we could tame this rotten swamp of a settlement. Hardly any of us had worked with his hands in his whole life!

William: It's not our fault, either! I don't think we could have known that we'd be holed up in a fort surrounded by enemies.

Nicholas: To be fair, we feel the same way, don't we? If any of us saw a Powhatan, we wouldn't be inclined to let them go without a fight.

Robert: I, for one, blame John Smith.

Nicholas: He's the only one not to blame! At least he tried–we were too lazy to go along. He made an awful lot of people angry just by being a good leader! And I find it very suspicious that that gunpowder exploded when it did. I think there were some in this colony who were awfully glad to see him need to return to England because of his injuries.

Robert: I still think it's John Smith's fault.

William: Well what happened after he left, then? Did things improve? No!

Thomas: George Percy happened then …

Nicholas: And we all know how that turned out.

William: John Smith at least knew how to talk to the Powhatan. Percy made a mess of negotiations.

Robert: As if that were the only problem. The drinking water here isn't even good, everyone has been getting sick, and not to mention a drought! Even if we knew what we were doing, how are we supposed to farm land when there isn't enough rain?

William: Not to mention that we didn't arrive in time to plant crops for the year …

Robert: Yes. Well, there's a reason we're calling it "the Starving Time," isn't there?

Thomas: Furthermore, there is the small matter of families …

Robert:	Small! Why if I could have a wife and family here, I'd be three times as motivated to get this place moving.
Thomas:	It *is* rather discouraging. Besides, it isn't fair that we have to do the cooking, baking, sewing … in addition to everything else. It's no wonder that we haven't been able to get things done around here.
Robert:	In any case, I can't wait to tell what's-his-name …
Nicholas:	Governor De La Warr.
Robert:	Yes, him … that we're leaving!
William: *looking over Robert's shoulder and nodding slightly*	Well, you'll have your chance now, because here he comes.
De La Warr: *stepping onstage with a ceremonial flourish*	My dear friends! I am very distressed to hear that you intend to leave the colony; is this true?
Robert: *looking rather startled, and with a remarkable change of tone*	I … indeed it is, Governor. We have had a very hard time of it here; no supplies, and so much death and sickness that we cannot imagine continuing. We wish to return to England.
De La Warr:	Gentlemen, I will not insult you by trying to convince you that you have not had hardship more than your share, and more than anyone should need to bear. But indeed, what awaits you in England? Many of you have sold your lands to seek your fortunes here. What if you were to find them? What if we could work together to transform this place into a haven for good and industrious men and women?
Thomas:	*And women?*
De La Warr:	Er, yes–and women, of course. There are women in England who share your spirit of adventure, and who would come here to live and work. We will establish families here; we will work together and make our fortunes here.
Thomas:	Well, when you put it that way …

William:	What about supplies? We have hardly enough to make it through the week, let alone to stay settled here.
De La Warr:	My ship is filled with supplies to provide you with relief from your suffering, and to help to hold us over until we have become self-sufficient.
Nicholas:	Well ...
De La Warr:	And I promise you the strong leadership that you have been lacking. I will not allow this colony to fail. If you can trust me to lead, I will make prosperous this settlement of Jamestown.
Robert: *turning aside and speaking privately with the other three colonists*	He certainly sounds confident ... what do you think?
William:	He had me at supplies.
Nicholas:	He had me at leadership.
Thomas:	He had me at families!
Robert:	Very well, sir; we will give our colony another chance. I assure you that we will do our best to work with you to give the colony the best chance of success.
De La Warr:	I am grateful to hear it, my friends. Now, onward–show me your place of settlement, and I will have the ship's crew help us to bring the supplies to the grounds.

Life in the Colonies

Objectives

- Study primary source documents of a variety of colonial figures.
- Infer circumstances and/or viewpoints based on available sources.
- Create a fictional dialogue based on close reading of available texts and sources.

Quest Document-Based Writing: Investigating Primary Sources

	Description	Duration	Materials	Participants
STEP 1 Set the Stage	Read a blackline master as an introduction to the project.	15 minutes	**Blackline Master:** Quest Kick Off	Whole Class
STEP 2 Launch the Activities	Divide students into small groups.	5 minutes	**Leveled Readers:** Life in the American Colonies; The Colonial People of the 1700s; The Colonial Experience: Voices From the 1700s	Small Groups
Activity 1 John Smith	Read a quote from and view a portrait of John Smith.	15 minutes	**Blackline Master:** Primary Source: John Smith, From *A Description of New England*	Small Groups
Activity 2 ELL Olaudah Equiano	Identify and write the main point of a quote from Olaudah Equiano.	20 minutes	**Student Activity Mat:** 5A The World **Blackline Master:** Primary Source: From *The Interesting Narrative of the Life of Olaudah Equiano, or Gustavus Vassa, the African*	Small Groups
Activity 3 Pocahontas	Study a portrait of Pocahontas.	20 minutes	**Blackline Master:** Primary Source: Pocahontas	Small Groups
Activity 4 Canassatego	Read and answer questions about a quote from American Indian Canassatego.	20 minutes	**Blackline Master:** Primary Source: From a Speech by Canassatego	Small Groups
STEP 3 Complete the Quest Prepare Your Script	Write a short script for a read-aloud.	45 minutes	Completed Quest materials	Small Groups
Read-Aloud	Read aloud scripts.	45 minutes		Small Groups
Answer the **Compelling Question**	Discuss the compelling question.	15 minutes		Whole Class

Quick Activities planner table

	Description	Duration	Materials	Participants
Map of the Slave Trade	Identify the routes of the colonial slave trade.	15 minutes	**Blackline Master:** Map of the Slave Trade, Steps in a Process A graphic organizer	Individual
Pie Chart of Ethnic Groups	Create a pie chart using statistics about ethnic groups in the colonies.	15 minutes	**Blackline Master:** Ethnic Groups in the 13 Colonies, 1775	Individual
American Indian and Colonial Conflicts ELL	Prepare and deliver a short presentation on a colonial-Indian conflict.	35 minutes	Classroom or Library Media Center resources	Small Groups
Colonial Founders Poetry	Write a poem about a colonial founder.	20 minutes	Classroom or Library Media Center resources	Partners
Salem Witchcraft Trials	Study the Salem witch trials and fill in a chart.	25 minutes	**Blackline Master:** Puritan Nonconformity	Small Groups
Finding Providence	Read and write a summary of a book about Roger Williams.	35 minutes	Classroom copies of Avi's *Finding Providence: The Story of Roger Williams*	Individual
Readers Theater: Begone, Roger Williams!	Perform a brief skit about the banishment of Roger Williams.	30 minutes	Script, props such as hats and clothing (optional)	Small Groups

Document-Based Writing: Investigating Primary Sources

Q^{**Compelling**}**uestion** ### Did everyone have the same rights during colonial times?

Welcome to Quest 4, Investigating Primary Sources. In this Quest, your students will study primary source documents and images in order to create a fictional dialogue, or "Read-Aloud," among certain historical figures. Their study of these sources will allow them to discuss the compelling question at the end of this inquiry.

Objectives

• Study a number of primary source documents that show a variety of points of view.

• Infer circumstances and/or viewpoints based on available sources.

• Create a fictional dialogue based on close reading of available texts and sources.

STEP 1   Set the Stage   ⏱ 15 minutes

Begin the Quest by distributing the blackline master **Quest Kick Off.** It will bring the world of the Quest to life, introducing a story to interest students and a mission to motivate them.

Story

The local historical society wants to stage a reading of a fictional meeting among several important and diverse figures from the colonies in the 1600s. They are commissioning a team to investigate and craft a script for what a dialogue between these figures might have looked like.

···

Mission

The local historical society has asked your students to study primary source documents and images in relation to certain figures from the seventeenth and eighteenth centuries and create a script for a fictional dialogue among them.

STEP 2 Launch the Activities

The following four activities will help students prepare for their script writing by allowing them to study the characters for which they will be writing. Note that all four can be done independently of the Quest.

You may assign the appropriate Leveled Reader for this chapter.

Divide students into small groups that will remain consistent for all the activities. Review the differences between primary and secondary sources.

Activity 1 John Smith (15) minutes

Materials: Blackline Master: Primary Source: From *A Description of New England*

Briefly introduce the fact that Captain Smith was a leader in the Virginia colony who did a great deal for the colony, but made enemies because of his strictness and his insistence that every man work hard for his living. Explain that the quote on the handout comes from writings he produced once he returned to England due to being wounded, and that he wished to eventually lead a new colony in New England. He therefore wrote of its virtues to convince people to finance his intended mission.

Distribute the blackline master **Primary Source: From *A Description of New England,*** which shows a portrait of John Smith and a vocabulary key.

Point out the spelling irregularities to the students. Explain that at the time of Smith's writing, English spelling was not yet standardized and that many documents from this time contain spellings and/or capitalizations that we would no longer recognize as being correct.

Students should study the handout and then in their small groups discuss the question: *How did Captain Smith view the colonies?* Students should be able to determine through discussion that he saw them as a land of opportunity and freedom to anyone willing to work for it. Circulate to monitor the progress of the groups' discussions. Remind students to keep in mind their mission and encourage them to begin to formulate ideas for John Smith's character in their scripts.

Materials: Student Activity Mat: 5A The World Blackline Master: Primary Source: From *The Interesting Narrative of the Life of Olaudah Equiano, or Gustavus Vassa, the African*

Provide some background information to students about the development of the colonial era slave trade, including the shift from indentured servitude to chattel slavery. Have students use the **Student Activity Mat: 5a The World** to review the various continents and countries involved in the slave trade including Africa, Caribbean area, and United States. Have students note that some enslaved persons were allowed by their "owners" to purchase their own freedom and that Olaudah Equiano had done so.

Distribute the blackline master **Primary Source: From *The Interesting Narrative of the Life of Olaudah Equiano, or Gustavus Vassa, the African,*** which contains an excerpt from a book by an enslaved man, Olaudah Equiano, after he gained his freedom.

Ask students to read the handout and then to write down what they think Equiano's main point is in this quotation. Students should conclude that he is decrying the treatment of African Americans in the colonies, whether free or enslaved and referencing injustice caused by racism.

 Support for English Language Learners

Reading: Give each student a copy of the blackline master **Primary Source: From *The Interesting Narrative of the Life of Olaudah Equiano, or Gustavus Vassa, the African.*** Have students look over the quote and vocabulary.

Entering: Read the quote from Equiano to students. Discuss each vocabulary term and then reread the quote. Ask students to explain the quote in their own words.

Emerging: Help students find the phrase that Equiano uses to mean *they are always afraid about losing their freedom.* Ask students what they think of when they hear the word *alarm.* (Possible answers: fire alarm, burglar alarm) Explain that the word *alarm* in this case is used to mean a very strong and present fear. Discuss the use of words to improve meaning.

Developing: Point out Equiano's use of the term *universally.* Ask the students whether they think that this term is meant literally, in that every single interaction with non-African Americans is negative, or figuratively (students should be able to determine that it is meant figuratively).

Expanding: Have students work in pairs to read the quote from Equiano. Ask students what impact the figurative use of the word *universally* has on the feel of the passage.

Bridging: Ask students to identify three vocabulary terms that imply something negative about free African Americans' experiences. (Possible answers: *nominal, plundered, mockery*) Discuss how each term affects the force and clarity of Equiano's overall message.

Activity 3 **Pocahontas** minutes

Materials: Blackline Master: Primary Source: Pocahontas

Review with students the founding of the Virginia colony, and the often tense and sometimes overtly hostile relationship between the colonists and the Powhatan Indian nation. Explain that the hostility was temporarily soothed when Pocahontas, the daughter of the chief of the Powhatan, married colonist John Rolfe in 1614.

Distribute the blackline master **Primary Source: Pocahontas**, which shows a portrait of Pocahontas painted while she was in England with her husband.

Explain that when Pocahontas married John Rolfe she moved with him to England. Encourage students to look at the manner in which Pocahontas (1596–1617) is dressed in the image. Students should recognize that she is dressed in European-style clothing. Explain that this image presents Pocahontas as being royalty, since she is the daughter of a chief. Its intent was to convey the sense that an American Indian could adopt a demeanor that was considered more European, and therefore more "civilized." If desired, emphasize the religious aspect of this view and point out that because European culture and religion were often very blended in the minds of Europeans, an adoption of European-style dress and social customs would be seen as also somewhat representing a conversion to Christianity (considered a desirable outcome by many Europeans).

Have the students study the image and answer the questions on the handout.

Activity 4 **Canassatego** 20 minutes

Materials: Blackline Master: Primary Source: From a Speech by Canassatego

Provide context for the handout by reviewing American Indian and colonial relations. Explain that even initially friendly relationships often soured.

Distribute the blackline master **Primary Source: From a Speech by Canassatego,** which shows a quote from the speech, as printed by Benjamin Franklin.

Have students read the quote from the handout and answer the questions. Discuss the answers as a class. Students should be able to determine that Canassatego is complaining about how the Iroquois have been treated while selling land and that he is insisting on only doing business when Brother Onas (presumably someone who had the trust of the Iroquois) is available. They should note that Canassatego is also complaining that the colonists are encroaching on land that is not theirs and that this unlawful settling has a negative impact on Iroquois hunting.

STEP 3 Complete the *Quest*

Part 1 Prepare Your Script (45) minutes

Materials: Completed Quest materials

Explain to students that they will be using what they have learned from the primary sources to write a script for a fictional discussion among the four historical persons represented by the four primary source handouts. Students should have access to the handouts during the script writing. Explain to students that the fictional discussion should address the following question:

What is your experience of being in or associated with the North American colonies?

Direct students to indicate the speaker by using the person's first initial followed by a colon (e.g., Olaudah Equiano would be represented as "O:," John Smith as "J:," etc.). Demonstrate on the board if necessary. Encourage students to consider the varying points of view they have heard and to let their characters dialogue with one another. If students need further guidance, refer them back to the original sources. Help them to compare the circumstances and attitudes of each. Each script should contain at least two instances of speech from each speaker. Review scripts after completion.

Part 2 Read-Aloud (45) minutes

Remind students that they are completing their mission by presenting their scripts as a Read-Aloud for the local historical society. If possible, have a local historian or member of the actual local historical society in attendance during the Read-Alouds. Each group should take turns reading their scripts, announcing beforehand to the audience which reader represents which speaker. After each script is read aloud, the class and/or audience can offer input as to what they noticed about how each character was portrayed.

Part 3 Compelling Question (15) minutes

After students complete their Read-Aloud, encourage them to reflect on what they learned. As a class, discuss the compelling question for this Quest: "Did everyone have the same rights during colonial times?"

Students have learned that history can be viewed from many perspectives. Encourage students to think about how a person's situation changes their perspective. They should use what they learned to answer the compelling question.

Quest

Name _____ Date _____

Investigating Primary Sources

The local historical society has decided to stage a reading of a short fictional discussion among several very different important people from colonial times. They need an investigative team to study primary source documents and images in order to faithfully imagine what a conversation among these figures might have looked like.

Your Mission

Your investigative team has been asked by the historical society to study primary sources and produce a script for a fictional discussion among the historical figures represented.

To help you write your script, you and your team will investigate the following:

Activity 1 **John Smith:** Read a quote from and study a portrait of Captain John Smith of Virginia.

Activity 2 **Olaudah Equiano:** Determine the view toward slavery of a former enslaved man.

Activity 3 **Pocahontas:** Study the portrait of an American Indian woman who married a Virginia planter.

Activity 4 **Canassatego:** Determine the circumstances to which an American Indian man is responding.

Complete Your Quest

Write your script and read it to the historical society, demonstrating your careful study of the primary source material.

🔍 Primary Source

John Smith, From *A Description of New England*

John Smith was the leader of the Virginia colonies until an injury forced him to return to England. Determined to return to North America, he led a voyage to the northeastern area of the Americas (New England) and wrote about the virtues of the places he saw. Ultimately, however, he was unable to find people willing to provide funding for him to start a new colony. Study the portrait and the quote below from Captain John Smith of the Virginia colonies.

> "Here every man may be master and owner of his owne labour and land. . . . If he have nothing but his hands, he may . . . by **industrie** quickly grow rich."
>
> —Captain John Smith, from *A Description of New England* (1616)

Vocabulary

industrie/industry, *n.,* hard work

Name _____ Date _____

Primary Source

From *The Interesting Narrative of the Life of Olaudah Equiano, or Gustavus Vassa, the African*

In 1789, the formerly enslaved Olaudah Equiano published his autobiography, which first detailed his kidnapping as a child in Africa and then his experiences as an enslaved person. He was taught to read and write under the direction of one of his masters (which was uncommon and potentially dangerous for an enslaved person). Later, he purchased his freedom from Robert King, his last master. Read the following quote from the autobiography of Olaudah Equiano.

Vocabulary:

hitherto, *adv.*, to this point
alarm, *n.*, worry
liberty, *n.*, freedom
nominal, *adj.*, in name only
plundered, *v.*, stolen from
redress, *n.*, justice
mildly, *adv.*, gently
mockery, *n.*, false presentation

Hitherto I had thought only slavery dreadful;

but the state of a free negro appeared to me now

equally so at least . . . for they live in constant

alarm for their **liberty;** and even this is but

nominal, for they are universally insulted and

plundered without the possibility of **redress.**

. . . In this situation is it surprising that slaves, when

mildly treated, should prefer even the misery of

slavery to such a **mockery** of freedom?

—Olaudah Equiano, from *The Interesting Narrative of the Life of Olaudah Equiano, or Gustavus Vassa, the African*, 1789

Name _____ Date _____

Primary Source

Pocahontas

Pocahontas was the daughter of Powhatan, or Wahunsenacawh, an Indian chief of the Powhatan. John Smith mentions her in his writings as being friendly toward the colonists and toward him especially. In April 1614, she married Virginia colonist John Rolfe and accompanied him to England. Study the image. Then answer the questions below.

Why do you think the artist wanted to draw Pocahontas?

_____

_____

What do you think Pocahontas might have been thinking during this portrait?

_____

_____

What do you think Pocahontas's family might have thought of the portrait?

_____

_____

From a Speech by Canassatego

Canassatego was a leader of the Onondaga nation, which was part of the Iroquois Confederacy. He was part of a group of Iroquois nations that made arrangements to sell American Indian land to the colonists of Pennsylvania. Read the quote. Then answer the questions.

> For the future we will sell no lands but when Brother Onas [the proprietor of Pennsylvania] is in the country; and we will know beforehand the quantity of the goods we are to receive. Besides, we are not well used with respect to the lands still unsold by us. Your people daily settle on these lands, and spoil our hunting . . .
>
> —Excerpt from speeches by Canassatego, an Iroquois, as printed by Benjamin Franklin, 1740s

1. What kind of situation do you think Canassatego is responding to in his speech?

   _____

   _____

2. Why do you think Canassatego wanted Brother Onas to be in the country during future land sales?

   _____

   _____

3. What attitude do you think these colonial trading partners might have had toward the American Indian nations?

   _____

   _____

Map of the Slave Trade

Individual (15) minutes

Materials: Blackline Master: Map of the Slave Trade, Steps in a Process A graphic organizer

Review the development of the slave trade with students, including the inhumane conditions suffered by captured and enslaved Africans.

Distribute the blackline master **Map of the Slave Trade,** which shows the trade routes that include the Middle Passage, and the graphic organizer Steps in a Process A.

Have students review the map. Discuss the circulation of tradeable goods as listed on the handout, explaining that enslaved persons were thought of as "goods." Have students fill in the Steps in a Process A graphic organizer. Starting with Europe, students should write in the steps involved in the slave trade. Students should be encouraged to note the cyclical nature of the slave trade.

Pie Chart of Ethnic Groups

Individual (15) minutes

Materials: Blackline Master: Ethnic Groups in the 13 Colonies, 1775

Review the concept of statistics and percentages with the students. Explain that statistics are a way of describing data, and that one way of expressing statistics is in the form of a pie chart. Demonstrate how to use statistics to create a pie chart by gathering some simple form of classroom data (such as student eye color), determining percentages, and filling in a pie chart on the board.

Distribute the blackline master **Ethnic Groups in the 13 Colonies, 1775,** which provides a blank pie chart and a set of statistics about colonial immigration.

Explain that between 1700 and 1775, the British colonies experienced an influx of people from around the world from many ethnic backgrounds. Explain that the statistics on their handouts are rough estimates of the percentages of immigrants who came to North America between 1700 and 1775 with the listed ethnic identities. Have students fill out the pie charts using the provided statistics. At the end of the activity, draw the pie chart on the board with input from the students.

American Indian and Colonial Conflicts

Materials: Classroom or Library Media Center resources

Each small group will be asked to conduct research using print and/or online resources on one of the following conflicts between American Indians and European colonists:

- Powhatan Wars

- Pequot War

- King Philip's War

- Lord Dunmore's War

Each group should prepare a short presentation based on their research. Students' presentations should include the dates of the conflict, the American Indian nations that were involved in the conflicts, the circumstances leading to the conflicts, the length of the conflicts, and the outcomes. When they have finished presenting, the groups should draw a timeline on the board and write down the dates of their assigned conflict in order. A class discussion can then take place concerning the progression of conflicts between colonists and American Indian nations.

Students can be directed to the following Web sites to help guide their research:

http://www.ushistory.org/us/2e.asp (Powhatan Wars)

http://colonialwarsct.org/1637.htm (Pequot War)

http://colonialwarsct.org/1675.htm (King Philip's War)

http://www.ohiohistorycentral.org/w/Lord_Dunmore%27s_War_and_the_Battle_of_Point_Pleasant (Lord Dunmore's War)

Support for English Language Learners

Speaking and Listening: Explain to students that when they present to a group, they can set up their information using tools such as an outline. Organizing information for presentations can be very helpful during the presentation itself. This activity will help students to practice organizing information.

Entering: Give a short "presentation" to the group concerning the steps required to clean the blackboard/whiteboard. Then go over each step with students, writing the steps on the board. Show students an outline and explain how to take the steps they helped you identify and put them in the outline. Ask pairs of students to use the outline to explain the steps required in the process.

Emerging: Give a short "presentation" to the class concerning the steps required to clean the blackboard/whiteboard. Once you have finished, have the students help you to write an outline of the information that you provided in the presentation. In pairs, have each student take turns giving their own version of the same presentation using the outline created by the class.

Developing: Ask students to help you list the steps involved in cleaning the blackboard/whiteboard. As you step through the process, have students record the steps. Then have pairs of students use the notes on the process to outline the steps. Ask students to use the outline to tell you the steps involved.

Expanding: Explain to students that you would like to prepare a presentation about how to properly clean the blackboard/whiteboard and why it is important to keep the board clean. Ask the students for their help in preparing an outline. Write the outline on the board. Then divide students into pairs, and have each student take a turn giving a presentation to the other based on the outline.

Bridging: Instruct students to create an outline for a short presentation on how to clean the classroom each day, and why it is important to keep it clean. Circulate to monitor progress. Have students divide into pairs, and have each partner deliver a presentation to the other based on the outline.

Colonial Founders Poetry

Partners (20) minutes

Materials: Classroom or Library Media Center resources

Students should be divided into pairs and asked to research the founders of one of the original 13 British colonies. Direct the students to collaborate to write a short poem to convey the basic information about who founded the colony and why it was founded. Encourage the students to use humor if desired. If the students would prefer to use shorter poetic forms, such as limericks or haiku, allow them to write several poems (enough to convey the necessary information) for the activity. These poems can then be read aloud to the class.

Salem Witchcraft Trials

Materials: Blackline Master: Puritan Nonconformity

Explain to students that while the Puritans had come to America looking for religious freedom, they did not tolerate religious differences within their own society. Then explain that the rigidity of social and religious norms can help us to understand the witchcraft hysteria in Salem Village that began in 1692.

Distribute the blackline master **Puritan Nonconformity,** which gives background about the trials and provides a chart for students to fill in. Place students in small groups.

As students read the handout, have them note that most of the accused were women. Explain that in Puritan society, women were not allowed the same personal freedoms as men. They were expected to follow an even more rigid set of societal and religious norms. Then have students use the following Web site to fill in the chart:

http://www.huntington.org/uploadedfiles/files/pdfs/lhthreligiousdissent.pdf

Explain that although the Salem witchcraft trials may be the most famous example of the use of the Puritan court system, other people had also experienced persecution at the hands of the Puritans, most notably Roger Williams (the founder of Rhode Island) and Anne Hutchinson. The above Web site also offers information about Anne Hutchinson, including a Readers Theater of her trial, which can be completed with students if desired.

Finding Providence

Materials: Classroom copies of Avi's *Finding Providence: The Story of Roger Williams*

Make the book *Finding Providence: The Story of Roger Williams* available to students for independent reading. If there are not enough copies for the class to read it at the same time, allow students to take turns.

When all students have finished reading, ask students to consider the effect that Roger Williams's banishment must have had on his family. Have each student write a short summary of the book. Encourage students to go over their summaries and edit them for clarity. If desired and if time permits, students can trade summaries with a partner to receive feedback and revise their summaries accordingly.

Map of the Slave Trade

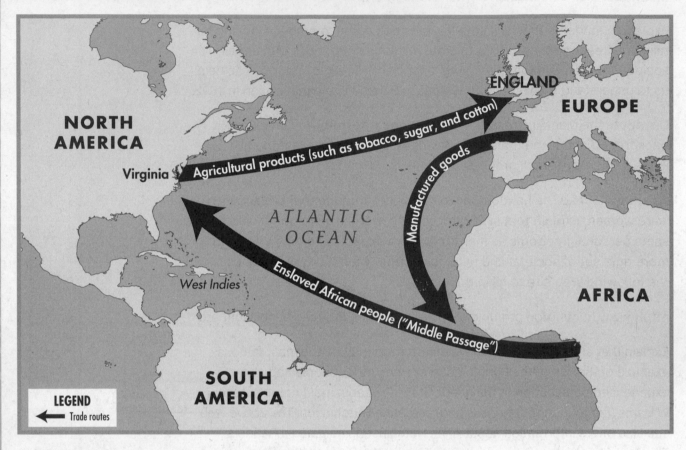

The Middle Passage is a name for the sea journey between Africa and North America for African people who had been captured to be sold into slavery. The Middle Passage was a part of a triangular set of trade routes that connected Africa, North America, and Europe. Study the map of the trade routes above, which include the Middle Passage.

FACTS:

The voyage from Africa to the colonies usually took about three weeks, but often took longer (up to about twelve weeks) in bad weather.

Captive persons were kept below deck and chained to keep them from rebelling against their captors.

The horrible conditions of the prisoners' captivity during the long voyage led to a great deal of sickness and death.

Name _____ Date _____

Ethnic Groups in the 13 Colonies, 1775

Between 1700 and 1775, the British colonies became the new home of immigrants of many different ethnic groups. Some of these people came here willingly, and others, like enslaved persons from Africa, unwillingly. The statistics below give a rough estimate of the percentages of immigrants who came to the colonies between 1700 and 1775 from different ethnic groups. Fill in the pie chart using the statistics below. Be sure to label the sections.

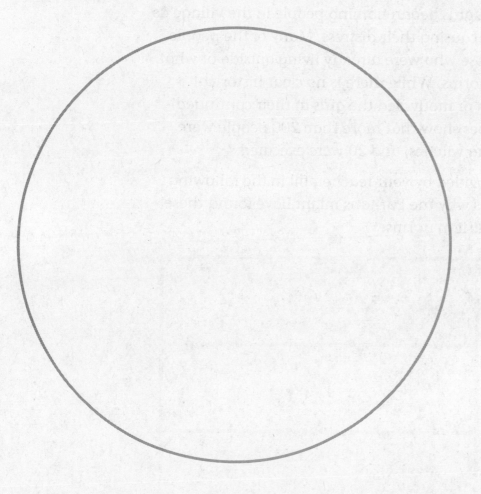

African: 47%

German: 14%

Irish: 18%

Scottish: 6%

English: 9%

Welsh: 5%

Other: 1%

(Based on information from *Migrations to the Thirteen British North American Colonies, 1700–1775: New Estimates* by Aaron Fogleman, *The Journal of Interdisciplinary History*, Vol. 22, No. 4 (Spring, 1992), pp. 691–709)

Puritan Nonconformity

The Salem witchcraft trials began in Salem Village, Massachusetts, in 1692. In Puritan New England, witchcraft was a crime punishable by death. The hysteria, or panic, began when one of the residents of the village, an enslaved woman named Tituba, led a fortune-telling session, which had left some young girls in Salem Village disturbed and behaving strangely. The inability of the doctor to determine a physical cause for the illness led to the belief that the girls were being tormented by witches. The girls began naming people in the village as specific persons who were causing their distress. Many of the people who were named were those who were already living outside of what were considered Puritan norms. While there is no clear historical consensus on what caused or motivated the girls in their continued accusations, the record does show that more than 200 people were ultimately accused of being witches, and 20 were executed.

Using the resources provided by your teacher, fill in the following chart, listing some reasons why the Puritans might have found these persons to be outside of Puritan norms.

Tituba	
Sarah Good	
Rebecca Nurse	
John Proctor	

Readers Theater
Begone, Roger Williams!

A story about the banishment of Roger Williams from the Massachusetts Bay Colony

---

The Parts

6 players:

- **Narrator**
- **Daniel Aldrich,** Massachusetts citizen
- **John Winthrop,** Governor of the Massachusetts Bay Colony
- **Nathaniel Thorne,** Massachusetts citizen
- **Richard Hayes,** Massachusetts citizen
- **Roger Williams,** banished Massachusetts citizen

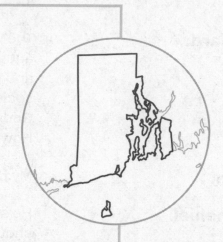

Director's Notes:

Nighttime in the town meetinghouse. The sky looks threatening, and a few flakes of snow have started floating down. A group of Massachusetts citizens, including Governor John Winthrop, have gathered to determine what to do with religious dissenter Roger Williams.

Narrator:	A meeting has been called by several important members of the Massachusetts Bay Colony. They have been having trouble with a minister by the name of Roger Williams, whose extreme views have caused problems.
Daniel:	Well, gentlemen, I'm sure I don't have to tell you why we are all gathered here this evening.
John:	I haven't been told yet, but you'd best hurry. The weather is making me uneasy, and I wouldn't be surprised to find that we have a blizzard on our hands before long.
Daniel:	For the time being, we have a different problem on our hands, a problem that goes by the name of Roger Williams.
John: *groaning*	Oh no.

Nathaniel:	He's been sick in bed. He can't be causing much mischief.
Daniel:	Well, as we all know, our courts served him with a sentence of banishment over his constant troublemaking over this idea of "religious freedom" that he is so fond of.
Richard:	The very idea! He would take away from the colony the authority to keep religious order. He thinks that religion and government should be kept separate—why, our whole society is founded upon being a chosen land, set apart by God and for God! Each nation must have its own church. How else will proper order be maintained?
John:	My dear friends, let us recall that he *is* a good Christian.
Nathaniel:	He's a separatist, not a Puritan, though! He doesn't think we should have anything to do with the Church of England.
Daniel:	To the point, gentlemen, to the point! When the courts banished him from the colony, we wanted to delay his sentence while he recovered from his illness, provided he stopped teaching. He has not done so. He continues to tell his visitors that he thinks that people should be free to practice whatever religion they like, without interference from the colony's government.
John:	But really, only in his own home . . .
Nathaniel:	In his own home or no, he is a public figure with a public sentence of banishment on his very public head! He ought to have known better.
Richard:	What do you propose?
Daniel:	Immediate banishment. And not simply out of the colony—I propose that we send him to England.
John:	To England!
Nathaniel:	That would serve him right, indeed; he has said some rather unfriendly things about the king, if I'm not mistaken. He will surely end up in prison, and that if he's lucky!
Daniel:	Are we agreed, gentlemen? To banish him for the glory of God and the protection of the religious authority of the state?
(All, in unison):	Agreed!

Richard: You were right about the weather, John—I think we had all ought to head home for now. I shall send the deputy to seize him upon the completion of what looks to be a nasty blizzard. Could be several days hence, by the looks of it. Well, goodnight all!

John:
looking rather uncomfortable

I shall be heading out shortly. There is one small matter I ought to take care of before I sleep tonight.

Narrator: John Winthrop did not head home because he needed to make a special stop. Loyal Massachusetts Puritan though he was, he felt it was his duty as a friend to inform a certain person of the goings-on at the meeting from that evening. And so he comes to the side of his ailing friend: Roger Williams.

Roger: Ah, John! Welcome! Have a cup of tea, the kettle is hot on the hearth still. I'm surprised you'd pick tonight to call, the sky—

John: Roger, we haven't time. I've just met with Daniel Aldrich, Nathaniel Thorne, and Richard Hayes. You've been banished, Roger—

Roger: Old news!

John: No, you've been . . . well . . . RE-banished, this time to England.

Roger:
with eyes wide, and turning pale

To England! But John, why?

John:
impatiently

Your foolish meetings here, Roger, that's why. You've been preaching your "religious tolerance" and criticizing the punishment of religious heretics by the civil authorities. You're a danger to the harmony of the colony, Roger! I wish you'd see sense.

Roger: If punishing men for their beliefs be sense, John, I'm afraid I neither have any nor wish to have it. It's you I pity more than myself. A government is not God's hand in the world, a church is, and a church must appeal to conscience, not to fear of burning, hanging, and humiliation.

John: Be that as it may—

Roger:
rising slowly and looking weak

Be that as it may, it is clear to me that as sick as I am, and as poor as the weather is tonight, I must get away at once.

John:

I don't know that you have a choice, but all the same—it is a cold night, Roger. How will you survive? You're still not well, and a blizzard is not a place for any man, let alone a sick one.

Roger:

I shall go south, my friend. There are some who can go with me and shall look after me as best they can. Perhaps someday I shall find a place where I can live out my ideal, where no citizen is denied justice or civil rights on the basis of his religion, where men and women may practice what they choose, and the church is freed to place its trust in God, and not in its own statesmanship.

John:

Roger, I disagree with you as heartily as I like you. May God be with you my friend, but I do warn you—do not come back here. Friend of yours though I am, I will not hesitate to bring you to justice if you again threaten our civil order.

Roger:

May God be with you all and have mercy upon your souls. I do beg you to reconsider your positions, and to allow—

John:
laughing

Upon the very doorstep of your departure, and still you are preaching—and to me, one who has helped to secure your banishment to begin with! Begone, Roger Williams, and trouble the Massachusetts Bay Colony no more. If you find your land, I shall wish you well, and perhaps someday God shall judge between us to say who was right.

Narrator:

Roger Williams left the Massachusetts Bay Colony that night. When the deputy came to bring him to England, he found the house empty. Roger Williams did find his land. He acquired it from the Narragansett Indians and founded a colony that attracted many religious dissenters. These dissenters included Anne Hutchinson, who would later be similarly banished from Massachusetts Bay. Roger Williams successfully implemented the first instance of the separation of church and state in the North American colonies. He named his land "Providence," and it has survived to this day as the capital of the present-day state of Rhode Island.

5 The American Revolution

Objectives

- Describe events leading up to the American Revolution.
- Identify key persons involved in the events.
- Recognize the importance of each event in the broader context of the pursuit of American Independence.

Quest Project-Based Learning: Revolutionary Timeline

	Description	Duration	Materials	Participants
STEP 1 Set the Stage	Read a blackline master as an introduction to the project.	15 minutes	**Blackline Master:** Quest Kick Off	Whole Class
STEP 2 Launch the Activities	Divide students into small groups and assign events.	5 minutes	**Leveled Readers:** Revolution in America; The Road to Independence; America's Fight for Independence	Whole Class
Activity 1 The Main Event	Find the main idea of the assigned event.	35 minutes	Main Idea and Details graphic organizer, **Student Activity Mat:** 3A Graphic Organizer; classroom or Library Media Center resources	Small Groups
Activity 2 Who Are They?	Identify 2–3 people involved in the event.	25 minutes	**Student Activity Mat:** 3B Time and Place **Blackline Master:** Persons of Interest, classroom or Library Media Center resources	Small Groups
Activity 3 ELL Write It Out!	Write text for timeline entry.	30 minutes		Small Groups
Activity 4 Illustrate!	Find or draw artwork for timeline entry.	25 minutes	Drawing tools, classroom or Library Media Center resources	Small Groups
STEP 3 Complete the Quest Assemble Your Timeline Entry	Assemble completed timeline entry materials.	15 minutes	Glue or glue sticks, scissors, cardstock or small pieces of poster board, masking tape or painter's tape	Small Groups
Deliver a Presentation	Groups present timeline entries and place on timeline.	35 minutes		Small Groups
Answer the **Compelling Question**	Discuss the compelling question.	15 minutes		Whole Class

Quick Activities

	Description	Duration	Materials	Participants
Benjamin ELL **Franklin's Inventions**	Research Benjamin Franklin's inventions.	30 minutes	Problem and Solution A graphic organizer, **Student Activity Mat:** 3A Graphic Organizer; classroom or Library Media Center resources	Small Groups
Women of the Revolutionary Era	Complete a matching activity about women of the revolution.	10 minutes	**Blackline Master:** Women of the Revolution, classroom or Library Media Center resources	Individual
Primary Source: *Common Sense*	Read and reword an excerpt from *Common Sense.*	30 minutes	**Primary Source:** *Common Sense*	Partners
Sons of Liberty Cartoon	View and answer questions about a political cartoon.	25 minutes	**Primary Source:** The Bostonians Paying the Excise Man	Partners
Readers Theater: The King's Dream	Perform a brief skit about King George dreaming he is present at the signing of the Declaration of Independence.	35 minutes	Script; props, such as quill pen (optional)	Small Groups

Project-Based Learning: Revolutionary Timeline

Q Compelling Question Was the American Revolution worth fighting for? Why or why not?

Welcome to Quest 5, Revolutionary Timeline. In this Quest, your students will prepare and deliver a short presentation about an event leading up to the American Revolution. Through their study of events leading to the revolution, they will be prepared to discuss the compelling question at the end of this inquiry.

Objectives

• Describe events leading up to the American Revolution.
• Identify key persons involved in the events.
• Recognize the importance of each event in the broader context of the pursuit of American independence.

STEP 1 Set the Stage ⏱ 15 minutes

Begin the Quest by distributing the blackline master **Quest Kick Off.** It will bring the world of the Quest to life, introducing a story to interest students and a mission to motivate them.

Story

The year is 1776. King Rex of the fictional country of Inquisitio is looking to offer fair and respectful leadership to his colonies. He has heard that the American colonists have started a revolution against British rule and he hopes to avoid a similar fate for Inquisitio and its colonies. King Rex and his advisors have decided to appoint a committee to create a timeline and discuss the sequence of events that led to the American Revolution.

Mission

Students have been commissioned by the king to create a timeline of events leading to the American Revolution, explaining how each event led to the overall break from British rule.

STEP 2 Launch the Activities

The following four activities will give students an opportunity to study events and persons related to the American Revolution. Note that all four can be completed independently of the larger Quest.

Divide students into small groups that will remain consistent for all the activities. Assign each group one of the following events leading to the American Revolution: the Stamp Act (1765), the Townshend Acts (1767), the Boston Massacre (1770), the Boston Tea Party (1773), the Coercive/Intolerable Acts (1774). You may assign the appropriate Leveled Reader for this chapter.

Activity 1 The Main Event minutes

Materials: Main Idea and Details graphic organizer, Student Activity Mat: 3A Graphic Organizer; classroom or Library Media Center resources

Have students use print and/or Internet resources to research their event. Books such as *Liberty!: How the Revolutionary War Began,* by Lucille Recht Penner, can be made available to students for this purpose. Instruct groups to take notes for their timeline entry. Distribute the graphic organizer Main Idea and Details or Student Activity Mat: 3a Graphic Oranizer to help students organize the information about their event.

Activity 2 Who Are They? minutes

Materials: Student Activity Mat: 3B Time and Place, Blackline Master: Persons of Interest, classroom or Library Media Center resources

Explain to students that they will be identifying two to three people who were involved in their event and collecting information about them.

Distribute the blackline master **Persons of Interest,** which shows a template for the student to enter information about the people they are researching. Students may also find it useful to use the timeline on the Student Activity Mat: 3B Time and Place to record information about each person.

Discuss how identifying the people involved in an event, and their overall points of view, can help us to better understand why the event proceeded as it did. Explain that recognizing the roles that individuals played in the events leading up to the American Revolution will help them to offer accurate information to King Rex.

Provide students with a variety of print and/or online materials to research two or three people involved with their event (students may have notes concerning involved persons from the research conducted during their previous activity; if so, allow students access to their notes). Have students conduct research and answer the questions on the handout. Explain that they will use the information from this activity when they write the event summary for their timeline entry.

Remind students that they are creating a timeline entry of their event and how it led to the American Revolution for King Rex. Encourage students to include information about the event itself and the people involved, while placing special emphasis on how the event affected the relationship between Britain and its colonies.

· ·

(ELL) Support for English Language Learners

Writing: Explain to students that when writing about an event, it is important to use connecting words that help to establish links between concepts and ideas. Remind students that when they write their summaries, they will need to show how each part of their assigned event is linked to the American Revolution.

Entering: Draw a picture of a house. Narrate to the students what you are doing using simple connecting words (e.g., *First, I draw the walls. Next, I draw the door. Finally, I draw the roof.*). Explain that the connecting words link the sentences together to describe the process. Ask pairs of students to write a three-part process using connecting words.

Emerging: Write the steps of a simple process such as making a sandwich, but write the steps in the wrong order. (e.g., *Spread mustard on the bread. Get out the bread. Put the pieces of bread together. Put meat and cheese on the bread.*) Then discuss with students how to use connecting words to put the events in order. Ask each student to write out a simple three- or four-part process.

Developing: Write these words: *First, Next, Then, Finally, Last, Later, Now, Next, During.* Explain that these words help connect ideas in time and help you keep track of steps or events. Have pairs of students write out a simple three- or four-step process using connecting words.

Expanding: Write these words and phrases: *Furthermore, Because of this.* Explain that these words and phrases help link concepts. Have each student write a funny story using the connecting words/phrases.

Bridging: Explain to students that in academic writing, more formal language is preferred. Write the phrase *because of this* on the board. Ask students to identify a more formal way of saying this. (Possible answers: *consequently, therefore*) Have them write a short paragraph using at least three formal connecting words/phrases.

Materials: Drawing tools, classroom or Library Media Center resources

Explain to students that since a timeline is a visual aid, the groups should provide illustrations that enhance their entries. Have the group determine the types of illustrations they would like to include. Students can use print and/or Internet materials to research period artwork (such as portraits or political cartoons) or draw their own illustrations.

Part 1 **Assemble Your Timeline Entry** ⏱ **15** minutes

Materials: Glue or glue sticks, scissors, cardstock or small pieces of poster board, masking tape or painter's tape (for timeline), completed Quest materials

To prepare for the timeline activity, place a long strip of masking tape or painter's tape along the board, classroom wall, or other appropriate area at a student-level height (this is the timeline). Divide into at least 12 segments, and label each segment with a year (from 1765 to 1776, or as desired for future classroom activities). Add notes as desired for events not researched by the students (such as the date of the signing of the Declaration of Independence). Be sure to leave enough space between years to allow for student entries.

Have students assemble their timeline cards, placing artwork and text onto a piece of cardstock or poster board. Remind them to write the date on the cards.

Part 2 **Deliver a Presentation** ⏱ **35** minutes

Remind students that they will be presenting their timeline entries to King Rex. Have each group present their card to the class. Remind them to state the date of the event. When each group has finished presenting, have the students place their cards along the timeline. Lead a class discussion concerning the progression of events. Explain how each event led to a growing sense of unrest in the colonies. If desired, leave the timeline displayed in the classroom as a reference tool for the duration of the study of the American Revolution.

Part 3 **Answer the Compelling Question** ⏱ **15** minutes

After students have placed their entries along the timeline, encourage them to reflect on what they learned. As a class, discuss the compelling question for this Quest: "Was the American Revolution worth fighting for? Why or why not?"

Students have learned about the progression of events in the colonies leading to discord with Britain and a growing desire to be independent. Encourage students to think about how the colonists began to view British rule. They should use what they learned to answer the compelling question.

Revolutionary Timeline

The year is 1776. King Rex of the fictional country of Inquisitio is looking to offer fair and respectful leadership to his colonies. He has heard that the American colonies in North America have started a revolution against British rule and he hopes to avoid a similar fate for Inquisitio and its colonies. King Rex and his advisors have decided to appoint a committee to create a timeline and discuss the sequence of events that led to the American Revolution.

Your Mission

The leader of Inquisitio has appointed your class to create a timeline of the events that led to the American Revolution. Research and prepare an entry for one of the major events to add to the timeline. You will present the timeline as a committee to King Rex and his advisors.

To prepare the timeline entry for placement on the timeline, work with your team to do the following:

Activity 1 | **The Main Event:** Research an event and take notes for your timeline entry.

Activity 2 | **Who Are They?:** Identify two to three people involved in the event and determine their views toward a revolution.

Activity 3 | **Write It Out!:** Write out the text for your timeline entry.

Activity 4 | **Illustrate!:** Choose the artwork to accompany your timeline entry.

Complete Your Quest

Assemble your entry and place it on the timeline. Then discuss its role in the sequence of events leading to the American Revolution.

Activity 2

Persons of Interest

Fill in the boxes for two to three people involved in your event.

Name: _____

Place of residence: _____

Role in event: _____

For/against revolution, and why: _____

_____

_____

_____

_____

_____

The American Revolution

Quest Student Worksheet

Quick Activities

Benjamin Franklin's Inventions

Small Groups (30) **minutes**

Materials: Problem and Solution A graphic organizer, Student Desk Map: 3A: Graphic Organizer; classroom or Library Media Center resources

Explain to students that Benjamin Franklin, known for his role in the Revolutionary War, was also a brilliant inventor. Divide students into small groups, and assign each group one of the following inventions: Franklin stove, long arm, bifocals, the lightning rod.

Have each group research the invention and prepare a short presentation to the class framed as a "sales pitch." The groups should collect and make use of whatever photographs and props they may need during the presentations.

Remind students that an effective sales pitch states a problem and then proposes the item being sold as the solution. Encourage students to emphasize how these inventions improved people's lives. Distribute the graphic organizer Problem and Solution A or the Student Activity Map: 3A Graphic Organizer to each group to help them visualize the information. Have groups present their sales pitch to the class.

ELL Support for English Language Learners

Speaking and Listening: Explain to students that a sales pitch is a form of advertising. The goal of a sales pitch is to convince someone that what you are trying to sell is useful to them.

Entering: Display for students a common object such as a ruler, notebook, or marker. Do a short sales pitch explaining why the item is useful. Then have students try to convince others in their group why an item they selected is something everyone wants.

Emerging: Show the students two objects that have similar, but not identical, uses (e.g., a pencil and a pen; a notebook and a sheet of paper). Have students choose the object that they feel is more useful and explain their choice.

Developing: Have small groups select a common classroom object and work together to come up with at least two reasons for their choice. Then the group should practice their arguments and present them to another group.

Expanding: Show students three classroom items that are important for daily use. Ask students which of the three objects they think is most important. Have each student provide at least three reasons to explain their choice.

Bridging: Choose a classroom item that is necessary for daily use. Tell students that you are considering getting rid of that item. Working in pairs, ask them to try to convince you to keep the item in the classroom.

Women of the Revolutionary Era

Individual (10) minutes

Materials: Blackline Master: Women of the Revolution, classroom or Library Media Center resources

Explain that women's roles changed during the course of the Revolution. Many men were serving as soldiers, and this often left women to manage family farms and business affairs alone. Women also traveled with the troops, providing cooking, laundry, and nursing services.

The new United States began to see the education of children in republican values as a primary civic duty. Educational opportunities for women slowly expanded to allow women to teach these values to their children. This duty came to be known as "Republican Motherhood."

Distribute the blackline master **Women of the Revolution,** which is a matching activity. Explain that the women listed on the handout were some of the most influential during the time of the Revolution. Have students use classroom or Library Media Center resources to help them match the names of the women to their descriptions.

Primary Source: *Common Sense*

Partners (30) minutes

Materials: Primary Source: *Common Sense*

Distribute the primary source **Common Sense,** which shows an excerpt from Thomas Paine's *Common Sense* (stating one of his reasons for opposing a monarchy) in chart form. Briefly review the difference between primary and secondary sources.

Explain that *Common Sense* was a pamphlet published in January 1776 that became immensely popular in the colonies and played a key role in winning over the public to the cause of independence from Britain.

Read through the entire quote with students, defining the following words and phrases (as they are used in the context of this quote) on the board:

- "composition of monarchy": the system of monarchy
- "means of information": way of getting information
- "highest judgment": excellent problem-solving skills
- "wherefore": as a result of which
- "unnaturally opposing": being in conflict with
- "character": nature of something

Have students work with a partner to go through the quote line by line and write each line in their own words.

Sons of Liberty Cartoon

Partners (25) minutes

Materials: Primary Source: The Bostonians Paying the Excise Man

Review the function of the Sons of Liberty in the American Revolution and their participation in the Boston Tea Party. Divide students into pairs.

Distribute the primary source **The Bostonians Paying the Excise Man,** which shows a cartoon drawn in 1774.

Have students review the handout, explaining that the cartoon depicts an actual event, namely the tarring and feathering of Boston Commissioner of Customs John Malcolm. (If students are not familiar with the concept of tarring and feathering, explain that it is a form of public humiliation that was practiced during this time.) Ask them whether the artist seems to approve of what the Sons of Liberty are doing (students should be able to determine that the artist does not approve). Then have the students answer the questions on the handout.

Women of the Revolution

Women made many important contributions during the Revolutionary War. After the revolution, women began to have an increased role in civic life. Teaching democratic ideals to children was seen as a civic duty. Women were given greater access to education so that they would be able to teach their children these ideals. This "Republican Motherhood," as it came to be called, had its roots in the contributions of women during the Revolutionary War.

Research the following women of the Revolution. Then match their names to the descriptions.

Abigail Adams	an enslaved young woman who learned to read and write and became the first African American woman to publish a book of poetry
Martha Washington	carried water to soldiers during the Battle of Monmouth and took her husband's place at his cannon when he collapsed during battle
Mary Ludwig Hays (Molly Pitcher)	known for her extensive correspondence with her patriot husband on social and political matters; also the second First Lady of the United States
Phillis Wheatley	one of the first significant female historians, who wrote an eyewitness account of the American Revolution
Mercy Otis Warren	accompanied her husband during the time the Army spent at Valley Forge; also the first First Lady of the United States

Common Sense

In 1776, Thomas Paine, a British immigrant to the colonies, published a pamphlet that criticized the British monarchy and certain forms of government. His pamphlet became immensely popular in the colonies. It is often credited with providing the necessary popular support for the American Revolution. Read the following excerpt from *Common Sense,* by Thomas Paine, and write each line in your own words in the space provided.

"There is something exceedingly ridiculous in the composition of monarchy;	
it first excludes a man from the means of information,	
yet empowers him to act in cases where the highest judgment is required.	
The state of a king shuts him from the world,	
yet the business of a king requires him to know it thoroughly;	
wherefore the different parts, by unnaturally opposing and destroying each other,	
prove the whole character to be absurd and useless."	

Name _____ Date _____

The Bostonians Paying the Excise Man

The Bostonians Paying the Excise Man is a British print by Philip Dawes that depicts the tarring and feathering of Boston Commissioner of Customs John Malcolm by the Sons of Liberty, a group that favored separation from England. Study the print and answer the questions below.

"The Bostonians Paying the Excise Man [tax man]" by Philip Dawes, 1774

NOTES

1. The victim is covered in tar and feathers, an extremely painful punishment.

2. The tree behind the men is the Liberty Tree, a symbolic meeting place for the Sons of Liberty.

Answer the following questions.

1. What does the ship in the background represent?

_____

2. What do the expressions on the faces of the attackers tell you?

_____

3. The Stamp Act is posted upside down on the tree. What do you think this might mean?

_____

4. What are the attackers pouring down the victim's throat?

_____

The Parts

- **King George III** of England
- **General George Washington** of Virginia
- **John Hancock**, Boston merchant
- **Thomas Jefferson**, writer of the Declaration of Independence
- **Benjamin Franklin**, statesman
- **Sebastian**, the King's attendant

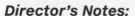

JULY 4, 1776

Director's Notes:

King George III of England has gone to bed after a long and frustrating day. The colonies have been weighing on his mind lately, as the American colonists seem unruly and defiant.

King:
yawning, and slowly standing up from his chair

Morning already? Couldn't be, I've only just gone to bed. And where am I? This is not my bedroom! You there, who are you, and what do you mean by disturbing the slumber of the King?

Washington:
stepping forward slightly from the opposite side of the stage

If by disturbing your slumber, you mean waking you from it, then I have done no such thing. Indeed, I am only here because you yourself have, in a sense, bidden it! You are dreaming, Your Majesty, dreaming about the American colonies.

King:

Dreaming! Well, I should expect that—I have had nothing but colonies, colonies, colonies on my mind for weeks! And about whom am I dreaming? Who are you?

Washington:

My name is George. George Washington at your service, Sir.

King: George indeed! Your name is familiar, though... Washington...You were a general in the war with France, were you not?

Washington: The same, Your Majesty. And I hope that I may do as much for my new country as I have done for my old.

King: Old country? New country? What are you talking about?

Washington: That is what you are here to find out.

Thomas Jefferson, Benjamin Franklin, and John Hancock walk onstage, but behind the two Georges. Washington and the King stand on either side of the stage, while the three Founding Fathers place a document on the table in front of them.

King:
becoming agitated

Here now, I demand to know the meaning of this...what is this meeting? Why are you all here? What's this that Washington is saying about a new country?

Jefferson: Well gentlemen, the document is now prepared. Who shall be the first to sign?

King: What document? What is he talking about?

Washington: He is talking about the Declaration of Independence.

King: What is that? I have never heard of such a document. Parliament has never passed any such thing.

Jefferson:
stepping forward and bowing slightly

Of course you have not heard of it, Your Majesty, for it is newly written. Allow me to introduce myself as its author: Thomas Jefferson, if you please. This document is a summary of the wrongs committed against us by the British Crown, a statement of our rights, and a declaration that all of our political ties to Great Britain are dissolved. We are henceforth a self-governing and independent nation.

King: The wrongs committed against you by the Crown? Do you mean the taxes levied in order to recover some of the cost of a very expensive war against the French to keep you colonies safe? It was British soldiers who fought for you then!

Hancock:

stepping forward, signing the document, and then turning to address the King

Allow me to be the first to sign! Your Majesty, these same soldiers which you say fought to defend us remained here afterward in times of peace, and by your own authority intruded upon us, requiring us to house and feed them in our private homes. Not to mention the horrific nature of the massacre that these British soldiers committed right in the city of Boston!

King:

A massacre, you say? You held a trial right here in the colonies for the soldiers involved in that altercation, and your own jury found all but one of them not guilty! I think that you, Mr. Hancock, may have been more concerned about your pocketbook than about the ideals of "liberty." My advisors tell me that you only took up a complaint against England after a ship of yours was detained for attempting to avoid a tax!

Hancock:

That may have been what initially drew me in to the cause, but why not? Both my countrymen and I believe these taxes to be both illegal and unfair. We are not represented in Parliament! Why should we have to pay a tax that we have had no say in approving? No taxation without representation!

Franklin:

Your Majesty, I too am signing this document.

King:

Benjamin Franklin!

Franklin:

Yes, it is I. You know, King George, that for many years, I have tried to speak to Parliament and to Your Majesty about the colonies, and how we needed more opportunity for self-governance. It is very different in the colonies than in England, and we needed the freedom to determine our own way. Had you cooperated, Your Majesty, it may have been that we would not have found ourselves in our current position. However, the dislike toward British rule is now at a level where I have no doubt, our only choice is to break from the Crown, and form our own country. A country friendly to our British brethren, I would hope, but our own all the same.

King:
groaning and holding his head as if he had a headache

This is no dream, this is a nightmare...

Jefferson:

Your Majesty, we believe that we have the right to break from England, to branch off on our own, to rule ourselves as we see fit. And we are willing to fight for that right.

Hancock:

No more of this intruding upon our affairs. If we are taxed, it will be a tax that we, the citizens, have approved.

Washington:

And Your Majesty, while I do not love war or bloodshed, I will do all within my power to ensure that the united colonies do not fail in their bid for independence.

King:

Treason—you are all guilty of treason!

Franklin:
turning toward the others

Well, gentlemen, we must all hang together now, or we must assuredly all hang separately!

All except King exit stage quietly. King slowly sits down, as if he were lying in bed, as he continues to talk, increasingly sleepily, to the characters in his dream.

King:

Treason! The colonies, independent.... declaration... treason... colonists... treason... treason...treason...

Sebastian:

Your Majesty, wake up Your Majesty! Your Majesty, I have some terrible news—the American colonists have declared their independence from England!

King:

Colonists? Independence? That's funny, I just had the strangest...Well! Gather my advisors, Sebastian! We will send the army—they will not get away without a fight while King George III is the king of England!

Objectives

- Describe the system of government set up by the U.S. Constitution.
- Understand the Preamble.

- Identify the Constitution's key supporters and opponents and describe their arguments.
- Explain why the Bill of Rights was added to the Constitution and summarize the rights it protects.

Quest Project-Based Learning: Present the Constitution

	Description	Duration	Materials	Participants
STEP 1 Set the Stage	Read a blackline master as an introduction to the project.	15 minutes	**Blackline Master:** Quest Kick Off	Whole Class
STEP 2 Launch the Activities			**Leveled Readers:** Writing the U.S. Constitution; We the People: The History of the Constitution; Checks and Balances: Creating the United States Government	
Activity 1 Rewrite the Preamble	Express the meaning of the Preamble.	20 minutes	**Primary Source:** The Preamble to the United States Constitution **Blackline Master:** In Your Own Words: The Preamble	Small Groups
Activity 2 Branches of Government Tree	Make a tree showing the branches of government.	30 minutes	**Blackline Master:** Branches of Government Tree **Student Activity Mat:** 3A Graphic Organizer **Video:** Capitol Visitor Center: At the Nation's Legislature Construction paper, scissors, tape or glue, markers	Small Groups
Activity 3 Checks and Balances Cartoon	Draw a political cartoon to illustrate checks and balances.	20 minutes	**Blackline Master:** Checks and Balances Cartoon	Small Groups
Activity 4 Advertise Freedom	Make a video ad to promote one of the amendments in the Bill of Rights.	30 minutes	**Leveled Readers**	Small Groups
STEP 3 ELL Complete the Quest Prepare Your Presentation	Prepare a presentation about the Constitution.	45 minutes	**Blackline Master:** Prepare your Presentation Presentation software; or large poster board, glue, and markers	Small Groups

Deliver a Presentation	Deliver a presentation to an audience.	45 minutes		Small Groups
Answer the **Compelling Question**	Discuss the compelling question.	15 minutes		Whole Class

Quick Activities

	Description	Duration	Materials	Participants
Moving West: Making a Decision	Use a map to help role play moving to the Northwest Territories in 1787.	20 minutes	**Blackline Master:** Moving West: Making a Decision	Small Groups
Write a Song About the Bill of Rights	Write lyrics to a song about the Bill of Rights and then perform it.	20 minutes	Classroom or Library Media Center resources	Small Groups
Create a Social Media Profile for Framers	Write a social media profile for one of the framers of the Constitution.	35 minutes	Classroom or Library Media Center resources	Small Groups
Constitution Matching Game	Create a vocabulary matching game.	10 minutes	Index cards	Partners
Debating: Federalists and Anti-Federalists	Research and prepare for a debate.	45 minutes	**Leveled Readers,** classroom or Library Media Center resources	Small Groups
Readers Theater: Philadelphia 1787 **ELL**	Perform a brief skit about the Constitutional Convention.	45 minutes	Script; Props, such as hats or clothing (optional)	Small Groups

Project-Based Learning: Present the Constitution

 **What makes a government work?**

Welcome to Quest 6, Present the Constitution. In this Quest, your students are asked to help the people of the imaginary country of Questopolis choose a new form of government and learn about democracy. The students will work in groups to create a presentation that tells the citizens about the U.S. Constitution and explain our form of government. The outcome is for groups to write and deliver a presentation about the Constitution. By completing the steps in the Quest, students will be able to discuss the compelling question at the end of this inquiry.

Objectives

- Describe the system of government set up by the U.S. Constitution.
- Understand the Preamble.
- Identify the Constitution's key supporters and opponents and describe their arguments.
- Explain why the Bill of Rights was added to the Constitution and summarize the rights it protects.

STEP 1 Set the Stage minutes

Begin the Quest by distributing the blackline master **Quest Kick Off.** It will bring the world of the Quest to life, introducing a story to interest students and a mission to motivate them.

Story

There has been a revolution in the fictional country of Questopolis. Queen Questia has been overthrown. Now the country must set up a new government.

....

Mission

Students have been chosen by the president of the United States to go to Questopolis. Their mission is to present the U.S. Constitution to the revolution's leaders as a model for a democratic system of government.

The following four activities will help students prepare for their presentations by researching the subject matter and creating visual aids. Note that all activities can be done independently of the larger Quest.

You may assign the appropriate Leveled Reader for this chapter. Divide students into small groups that will remain consistent for all the activities.

Activity 1 **Rewrite the Preamble** (20) minutes

Materials: Primary Source: The Preamble to the United States Constitution, Blackline Master: In Your Own Words: The Preamble

Explain to students that they will read the Preamble to the United States Constitution. Remind them of what a constitution does, and review how our Constitution was written. Define primary and secondary sources for students, and ask them to determine which category the Preamble falls into.

Distribute the blackline masters **Primary Source: The Preamble to the United States Constitution** and **In Your Own Words: The Preamble,** which show the text of the Preamble and present the activity. Have students read the Preamble aloud to one another and fill in the chart.

Finally, have students rewrite the Preamble in their own words on a separate piece of paper. For example, they may rewrite the phrase "ensure domestic tranquility" to read "make sure the country is peaceful."

Activity 2 **Branches of Government Tree** (30) minutes

Materials: Blackline Master: Branches of Government Tree, **Student Activity Mat:** 3A Graphic Organizer, Video: Capitol Visitor Center: At the Nation's Legislature, construction paper, scissors, tape or glue, and markers

Provide students with construction paper, scissors, markers, and tape or glue. Explain that students will be making a tree showing the branches of government.

Distribute the blackline master **Branches of Government Tree,** which lists the branches of the U.S. government and the roles they play in governing the United States, and **Student Activity Mat:** 3A Graphic Organizer. Suggest students use the Student Activity Mat to take notes as they learn about the branches of government.

Before they begin, you may want to assign the video **Capitol Visitor Center: At the Nation's Legislature.** Then, review the executive, legislative, and judicial branches of government. Remind students that each has its own role and powers.

Have students study the chart on the handout to prepare for the activity. Then, have them create a tree with three branches out of construction paper and glue. Label the branches with the names of each branch of government. Then have students make two leaves for each branch. On each leaf, instruct students to write down one way that branch is important.

Activity 3 | Checks and Balances Cartoon 20 minutes

Materials: Blackline Master: Checks and Balances Cartoon

Distribute the blackline master **Checks and Balances Cartoon,** which has an example of a political cartoon as well as questions designed to help the student identify the features of a political cartoon.

The handout asks students to identify three key features of the cartoon: the image, the small explanatory labels, and the main tag line. Note that the abbreviations do not match those we use today.

Circulate to help groups interpret the cartoon and identify these features, or complete this part of the activity as a class.

Then, review the concept of checks and balances in our Federal government with students. Explain that each of the three branches of government has the power to check, or stop, other branches from abusing their powers. Give examples, such as the President's power to veto a law or the Supreme Court's power to rule that a law is unconstitutional.

Explain that checks and balances are an important part of our system of government. As a class, have students generate a list of benefits they provide.

Finally, have students work in their groups to create their own cartoon illustrating the concept of checks and balances. Encourage groups to divide the task into parts such as sketching, coloring, and writing, and assign one role to each member.

Activity 4 | Advertise Freedom 30 minutes

Materials: Leveled Readers

Assign the appropriate Leveled Reader for this chapter.

As a class, ask students to describe video advertisements they have seen on television or online. Write down on the board elements they have in common, such as the use of music or humor. Explain that students will be making their own TV ad to promote one of the amendments in the Bill of Rights. Review the Bill of Rights with students. Remind them that it was added to persuade opponents to ratify the Constitution.

List the important rights it protects, and discuss as a class how life in the United States might be different if these rights were not protected.

Have students work in their groups to write and stage their ad. If possible, have them record their ad to play as part of their presentation. Or alternatively, they may act out their ad as part of their presentation.

Part 1 Prepare Your Presentation ⓐ45 minutes

Materials: Blackline Master: Prepare Your Presentation; presentation software or large poster board, glue, and markers

After students have completed the Quest activities have them prepare for and deliver their presentations. Distribute the blackline master **Prepare Your Presentation,** which guides students through this process.

You may wish to have each group create a digital presentation with slides for each of their points. They can include photos of their illustrations and their rewritten Preamble, as well as a video recording of their ad.

Alternately, you may have students post their illustrations on large poster board, act out their ad as part of the presentation, and read aloud their Preamble.

Remind students about the Quest mission. Students should recall that they are talking to the leaders of Questopolis. How can they best explain our Constitution? What are the most important points to get across?

ⓔⓛⓛ **Support for English Language Learners**

Speaking and Listening: Review some elements that distinguish formal and informal language. Explain that sentence fragments and words with English roots are less formal than full words, complete sentences, and words with Greek and Latin roots.

Entering: Explain to students that sometimes we use more formal language in class or when making a presentation. Help two to three students role-play talking about what they want to do after school today. Then have them role-play asking the principal for extra recess time. Discuss the different types of language they might use.

Emerging: Divide students into pairs. Have students role-play as two friends making a plan for the weekend. Then have them role-play a teacher asking a student a question in class and the student responding. Remind students to use more formal language in the second scenario. Have students write down three formal words they might use in their presentation.

Developing: Ask one student to tell about something fun they did recently. Then ask another student in the group to retell the story using more formal language. Then have other students repeat the activity. Discuss the different types of language that were used and how they change the way the story sounds.

Expanding: Divide students into pairs. Encourage one partner to tell a story about a recent funny or interesting event. Have the other partner retell it in formal language. Then have the partners switch roles. Have students write down five formal words they might use in their presentation.

Bridging: Tell a story to students using everyday, informal language. Then read aloud a paragraph from a newspaper or magazine article in a formal tone. Have students point out the differences in language between the story and the article. Have students write down seven to ten formal words they might use in their presentation.

Part 2 Deliver a Presentation minutes

If possible, set up a real-life audience of classmates, parents, or community members. Consider distributing the blackline master **Quest Kick Off** to the audience before the presentations so they are familiar with the story and mission of this Quest.

Part 3 Compelling Question minutes

After students deliver their presentation, encourage them to reflect on what they learned. As a class, discuss the compelling question for this Quest: "What makes a government work?"

Students have learned about different aspects of the Constitution, including the branches of government and checks and balances. Encourage students to think about how these help our government function. They should use what they learned to discuss the compelling question.

Capital City Times
BREAKING POLITICS ENTERTAINMENT BUSINESS SPORTS **MENU**

REVOLUTION!

CAPITAL CITY, QUESTOPOLIS – Last night, Queen Questia fled from her palace and left the country. This follows weeks of protests. Thousands of citizens had taken to the streets of Capital City. They demanded that Questopolis become a democracy.

But what kind of government will the protesters build? The revolution's leaders have asked the president of the United States for help. The president has sent experts to teach them about the U.S. Constitution. Will their presentation convince the people of Questopolis to choose democracy? Or will a dictator take power?

Your Mission

The president of the United States has picked you and your team to go to Questopolis. You will teach its people about the U.S. Constitution by giving them a presentation.

To prepare and deliver your presentation, work with your team to do the following:

Activity 1 **Rewrite the Preamble**: Read the Preamble. Then, analyze it and put it into your own words.

Activity 2 **Branches of Government Tree:** Use art supplies to make a tree made up of the three branches of government.

Activity 3 **Checks and Balances Cartoon:** Draw a political cartoon about checks and balances.

Activity 4 **Advertise Freedom:** Create a TV ad for one of the amendments that makes up the Bill of Rights.

Complete Your Quest

Write and deliver your presentation, explaining what you have learned about the Constitution.

Name _____ Date _____

The Preamble to the United States Constitution

Introduction

A preamble is the introduction to a document. It explains the document's purpose. Below is the Preamble to the United States Constitution. As you read it, use the vocabulary and definitions to help with difficult words.

Vocabulary

domestic, *adj.,* at home, inside the country

tranquility, *n.,* peace

defence/defense, *n.,* protection, especially from war

welfare, *n.,* well being

liberty, *n.,* freedom

posterity, *n.,* future

"We the People of the United States, in Order to form a more perfect Union, establish Justice, ensure **domestic Tranquility**, provide for the common **defence** [defense], promote the general **Welfare**, and secure the Blessings of **Liberty** to ourselves and our **Posterity**, do ordain and establish this Constitution for the United States of America."

Fun Fact

The United States Constitution has **4,543** words.

India has the world's longest constitution, with **146,385** words.

In Your Own Words: The Preamble

Read the Preamble to the United States Constitution. It
states six goals for what the Constitution is meant to do.
Fill in the missing goals below in the first column. Then use
the second column to restate the goal in your own words.

Goal	Meaning
form a more perfect union	
ensure domestic tranquility	keep peace in the country
secure the blessings of liberty	

Now, take the meanings you wrote in the chart and use them
to help you rewrite the whole Preamble in your own words. Use
plain language that is easy to understand. Try to emphasize the
full meaning of the Preamble.

Name _____ Date _____

Branches of Government Tree

You know that trees have many branches. When we talk about our government, we say that it has three branches. What do we mean?

The branches of government are its parts. Like the branches of a tree, they are separate from one another. But also like tree branches, they all form part of a whole.

Each branch of government has its own role and its own set of powers. This helps make sure that no one part of the government can misuse its power.

Study this chart, which shows the three branches of our federal government.

Branch	Who is it?	What does it do?
Legislative	Congress	Makes laws
Executive	The president and those who work for him or her, such as members of the military	Enforces laws to make sure people follow them
Judicial	The Supreme Court and other courts	Interprets laws and decides if they follow the Constitution

Now follow your teacher's instructions to create a Branches of Government Tree. Include and label all three branches on your tree. Then, add two leaves to each branch to list details about what makes each branch important.

Checks and Balances Cartoon

This political cartoon was created by Benjamin Franklin before the American Revolution. It urged people in the British colonies in America to join together to fight a common enemy: the French. Later, the colonies would join together to fight the British. The abbreviations in the cartoon represent the colonies.

Benjamin Franklin. "Join, or Die." Cartoon

Many political cartoons use similar features to get their points across. Find the following in this cartoon:

- Circle the main image in the cartoon.
- Put a star next to one of the small labels that helps to explain the image.
- Draw a rectangle around the main tag line, or a clever line of text that sums up the point of the cartoon.

What does the snake represent in this cartoon?

_____

Who should join or die?

_____

On a separate piece of paper, draw your own political cartoon to promote the idea of checks and balances. Remember that this is a principle of the government set up by the Constitution. It means that each of the three branches of government can check, or limit, the power of the other branches.

Quest Findings

Name _____ Date _____

Prepare Your Presentation

You have studied the U.S. Constitution. Now, it is time to show what you have learned. Remember that your mission is to give a presentation about the Constitution to the leaders of the revolution in Questopolis so that they can see a model for how a democracy can work.

Time to get to work!

1. To prepare your presentation, think about its purpose and audience. Who is the audience for your presentation?

_____

What is the main goal of your presentation?

_____

2. Write down a list of the main points you plan to make in your presentation.

•	_____ _____
•	_____ _____
•	_____ _____

Quick Activities

Moving West: Making a Decision   Small Groups ⟨20⟩ minutes

Materials: Blackline Master: Moving West: Making a Decision

Tell students that the Treaty of Paris ended the American Revolution. According to its terms, the United States gained territory west to the Mississippi River. After the war, the U.S. government had to organize this land. The first land that Congress organized was the Northwest Territory.

1. Divide the class into groups each containing two to four students.

2. Distribute the blackline master **Moving West: Making a Decision** which shows a map of the Northwest Territory in 1787 and contains short-answer questions for the students.

3. Have students pretend they are farmers moving to the Northwest Territory from one of the thirteen states.

4. As they study the map, have them answer the questions on the handout, decide where in the territory they want to move, and mark their destination with an X.

5. Have students use the scale of miles/km to measure the distance from their state to their destination.

6. Finally, have each group explain its choice to the class.

Write a Song About the Bill of Rights   Small Groups ⟨20⟩ minutes

Materials: Classroom or Library Media Center resources

Organize students into small groups. Have them research a list of key ideas and terms associated with the Bill of Rights, the first ten amendments to the U.S. Constitution.

Ask each group to think of a popular song they like and have them write new words to that song that reflect what they have learned about the Bill of Rights. The song should aim at educating younger children about the Bill of Rights. Then, have the groups perform their songs for a younger grade class and ask the younger students to vote on the most creative song.

Create a Social Media Profile for the Constitution's Framers

Small Groups 35 minutes

Materials: Classroom or Library Media Center resources

Divide students into small groups and assign each group one of the framers of the U.S. Constitution:

> George Washington, Alexander Hamilton, Benjamin Franklin, James Madison, Patrick Henry, Edmund Randolph, William Paterson, Roger Sherman

Provide students with resources about the framers and their role in the creation of the U.S. Constitution. Then have students create social media posts that include some or all of the following: name, state represented, spouse and children, early career or job, personal wealth, and slave ownership status. Then write two "posts" that have to do with the person's role in the Constitution, and include one or two images of the person (these can be drawn or from the Internet).

When students have completed their social media pages, you may wish to display them in the classroom or in the hallway.

Constitution Matching Game

Partners 10 minutes

Materials: Index cards

Have each student work with a partner to write the following words and definitions on one side of the index cards. Each card should have either one word or one definition, not both.

delegate	a representative
veto	to refuse to approve something
amendment	a change or improvement
compromise	a situation when groups on each side of an issue each give in a little to reach an agreement
Preamble	the introduction to the Constitution of the United States

constitution	a written plan for government
separation of powers	the idea that the powers and duties of government are divided among separate branches

Mix all the cards and lay them in rows face down. One student turns over any two cards. If the term and definition match, the student keeps the cards. If they don't match, he or she turns them back over and the other student tries to find a match. The game continues until all cards have been matched. The player with the most matches wins the game.

Debating: Federalists and Anti-Federalists

Small Groups 45 minutes

Materials: Leveled Readers, classroom or Library Media Center resources

Tell students that in the spring and summer of 1787, delegates from each state met in Philadelphia for a Constitutional Convention. They drafted a new constitution, creating a form of government that satisfied many but not all the delegates. Discuss the differences between the opinions of the Federalists and the Anti-Federalists and how this affected ratification. Assign the appropriate Leveled Reader for this chapter.

Federalists	Anti-Federalists
Supported the Constitution; supported a strong federal government	Opposed the Constitution; feared a strong federal government; wanted a Bill of Rights

Disagreements between Federalists and Anti-Federalists became heated. Assign students into two groups: Federalists or Anti-Federalists, and explain that the sides will participate in a mock debate.

If you have a large class, you may want to further divide the class and hold several debates. Give students time to research their positions. Appoint students, yourself, or other teachers as moderator(s) for the debate.

Set up and share rules for the debate. Rules may include the amount of time permitted to speak and refute, and time for closing arguments. You may wish to invite another class or members of the faculty to watch the debates.

Readers Theater: Philadelphia, 1787

Materials: Script, props (such as hats or clothing; optional)

The students will be performing a short skit on the Constitutional Convention. This skit has a total of seven speaking roles. Divide the class into small groups, and assign or have students select the roles that they will play.

Distribute the blackline master **Readers Theater: Philadelphia 1787**, which are the pages of dialogue for a brief skit about the Constitutional Convention.

If desired, give the students time to look over the script, research the characters, and make or obtain any props that they would like to use. Remind students to speak clearly and at an understandable pace during the skit. Have the students perform the skit in their small groups.

ⓔ Support for English Language Learners

Speaking and Listening: Remind students that active listening will help them to recognize and reinforce vocabulary, sentence structure, and idioms. Remind students to listen carefully to the dialogue in the skit, and encourage them to ask questions if there are words or expressions that they do not understand.

Entering: Write the following words on the board: *big, huge, massive, enormous.* Say each word for students and discuss the meaning of the words. Help students understand the subtle differences between the words. Repeat with the words: *small, little, tiny, minuscule.*

Emerging: Have one student say aloud the sentence *That rock was so massive that I could not pick it up.* Have the students guess the meaning of the word *massive* based on the context of the sentence. Ask students to use a thesaurus or dictionary to find two more words that also mean *big,* and have each student repeat the sentence using one of those words in place of *massive.*

Developing: Work with a small group and write this pair of sentences on the board: *Ava told a funny joke. Ava told a hilarious joke.* Discuss the sentences and review what *hilarious* means. Then ask each student to write two sentences that mean basically the same thing.

Expanding: Divide students into pairs. Say: *My fiery temper gets me in trouble, because when I am angry I say things that I do not mean.* Ask students to note the use of the adjective *fiery* in this context. Explain that it is figurative language, referring to the intensity of feeling as symbolized by the intense heat of fire. Ask students to each write three sentences describing strong emotions using adjectives, then have students share their sentences.

Bridging: Divide students into small groups. Assign each group one of the following idiomatic phrases: *spill the beans, bent out of shape, chip on one's shoulder, beat around the bush,* and *bite the bullet.* Have each group look up the meaning of the phrase, and then use the phrase in a sentence. Have each group share their sentence.

Moving West: Making a Decision

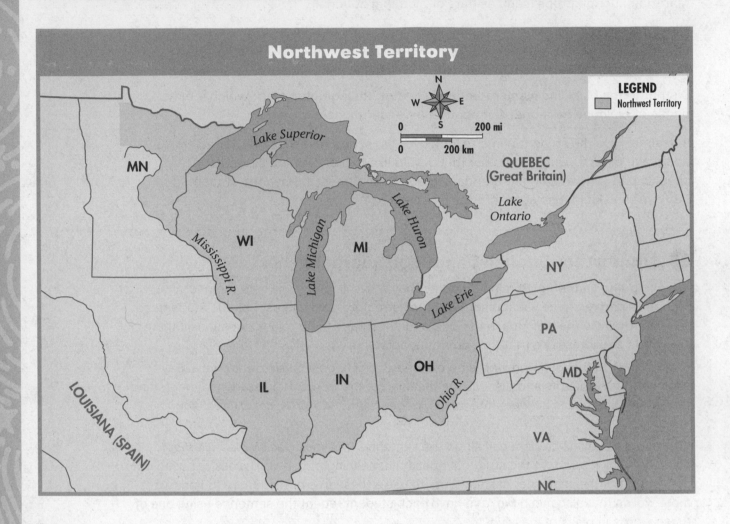

Northwest Territory

LEGEND
Northwest Territory

In September 1783, the United States and Great Britain signed the Treaty of Paris, ending the American Revolution. According to the treaty, Great Britain agreed to grant some land it controlled to the United States. This land stretched from the Appalachian Mountains to the Mississippi River. Of these vast lands, the first portion that Congress organized was the Northwest Territory. This land is located in the northern part of the territory and is shown by the gray shaded area. The borders and abbreviations in this region are present-day borders and names of states.

Where in the new territory will you move? Study the map and answer the questions on the next page. Then make your decision.

116

Name _____ Date _____

Imagine that it is the year 1787, and you are a U.S. farmer living in one of the eastern states. You want to move your family to the Northwest Territory where there is a great deal of land. The land is not empty. There are American Indian nations living on the land. Remember that there are no trains, trucks, or highways in 1787.

1. What rivers and lakes are located near the Northwest Territory?

_____

_____

2. Will you ship the products from your farm by water or by land?

_____

_____

3. Which nations control land near the Territory?

_____

_____

4. Where in the Northwest Territory would you move to and why? Put an **X** on the map to mark the place you chose.

_____

_____

5. Choose one of the eastern U.S. states shown on the map (this will be your starting location). Use the map's scale to measure the distance between a location in the state and the location you chose in the Northwest Territory.

Write the state you measured from _____ and the

approximate location of the area where you measured to _____.

Write your measurement here _____.

A story about how citizens in Philadelphia may have debated the issues in 1787.

The Parts

5 players:

- **Narrator**
- **Barnabus Dawkins,** former Continental soldier, wounded in war
- **Abigail Dawkins,** Barnabus's wife
- **Elijah Johnson,** printer at the *Pennsylvania Gazette*
- **Henrietta Johnson,** Elijah's wife

2 additional players—during the improvisation:

- **Benjamin Franklin,** Delegate to the Constitutional Convention
- **George Washington,** President of the Constitutional Convention

Director's Notes:

The play is scripted during a day of the Constitutional Convention, which is taking place in the Pennsylvania State House in Philadelphia in June 1787. Outside the convention, a small group of friends is discussing what might be happening inside. After the session ends, two of the convention members, George Washington and Benjamin Franklin, leave the building and slowly pass by the group. Eager to hear news about the convention, the group hopes to engage America's founders in a lively conversation. This is the time when the actors can improvise their parts. (You may wish to conduct additional research beforehand.)

Narrator: It is a hot and humid summer day in late June 1787. State delegates are meeting inside Philadelphia's Pennsylvania State House to discuss how they can make the national, or federal, government stronger and more effective. Barnabus Dawkins and his wife Abigail are standing outside the State House, eagerly awaiting the outcome of the meeting. They are with their friends, Elijah and Henrietta Johnson.

Abigail
fanning herself to stay cool

I cannot believe that the State House windows are shuttered in this terrible heat! How can the delegates think, let alone debate the issues?

Barnabus:
leaning on a cane to support his leg

It most certainly will get hotter in the meeting room because tempers are aflame! Delegates are divided over who should be more powerful—the federal government or the individual states.

Henrietta:

I wish we could find out what is going on. It is not fair that the delegates are in a secret meeting. We have a right to know what they are deciding about our future.

Elijah:
wiping the sweat from his brow with a handkerchief

I agree, my dear. I do hope that we can keep the Articles of Confederation. It has mostly worked for the past six years. It just needs to be strengthened a bit. We must make sure that each state keeps its power.

Barnabus:

I'm afraid I disagree with you, my friend. We need a new constitution and a new plan for our nation's government. Our country has been in debt since the war—we owe far too much money. I, and many of the soldiers who fought in it, never received the pay that was due us.

Abigail:

Our currency, the "continentals," is almost worthless. And our federal government has limited powers and cannot collect taxes. It is at the mercy of each state to give it money.

Henrietta:

That may be true. But if we have a stronger federal government, are you not afraid that the president could become like the king of England and have too much power?

Barnabus:
vehemently tapping his cane on the ground to emphasize his point

No, no, no. That would never happen! First of all, the president of the convention, George Washington, fought for our country's independence. He is not one who is hungry for power. Secondly, he understands that we need a strong federal government, one that has an army to prevent what happened last year.

Abigail:
looking perplexed

What are you referring to, Barnabus?

Barnabus:
eyebrows raised

Do you recall when Massachusetts raised its taxes?

Elijah:
nodding his head vigorously

Of course! Many farmers lost their land and some even went to prison.

Henrietta:
also nodding

Yes, I remember now. Daniel Shays, a farmer and former soldier in the Continental army, led a group of men to shut down the highest court in the state.

Abigail:
fanning herself

He and his men tried to steal weapons from our nation's weapons depot. Luckily, they failed.

Barnabus:
raising his index finger to make a point

That is a fact! This rebellion never would have happened if we had a strong federal government, and a federal army to boot!

Elijah:
wiping his brow again

I must disagree with you—and agree with the brilliant Virginia speaker and Revolutionary War hero, Patrick Henry. Unfortunately, he is not at the convention to state his case. He refused to attend because he will not even consider a new constitution.

Henrietta:
sighing

You are right, Elijah. He—like you and me—believes that the states should keep their power.

Barnabus:
lowering his voice

There are rumblings that delegates want an entirely new form of government with three separate branches.

Elijah:
whispering

What do you mean?

Barnabus:

I am talking about a government that has one group make laws, another group carry out the laws, and a third group to decide what each law means.

Abigail:

That is an interesting idea, indeed!

Henrietta:	Rather than giving the federal government all of the power, or the states having too much power, do you think there could be some sort of a compromise?
Elijah: *rubbing his chin in thought*	Hmmm. A compromise might work, if the states could keep some of their power. I am sure our leaders are debating that issue as we speak.
Barnabus: *holding up his cane and pointing it toward the State House*	Look! The meeting has adjourned.
Abigail: *excitedly pointing*	I see George Washington!
Henrietta: *smiling*	He is walking this way… with Benjamin Franklin! Do you think they would stop to talk with us?
Elijah: *waving his handkerchief to get the attention of the Founding Fathers*	I have met Mr. Franklin because of my newspaper work at the *Pennsylvania Gazette*. Let me see if they will come over to talk with us. Sir…Mr. Franklin? How are you?
Benjamin Franklin:	Hello, my good man! I cannot discuss the details of our meetings, but exciting changes are coming to our United States.

George Washington nods in agreement.

(Washington and Franklin continue on their way, conversing quietly until offstage and the four citizens continue in an opposite direction continuing an improvisational conversation until offstage. Only the Narrator is left.)

Narrator:	The Constitutional Convention created a new U.S. Constitution with a new form of national government with three branches. It had checks and balances so that no branch gained more power than the other. The Constitution also divided power between the national government and the state governments. It is the same form of government in use today.

(Narrator leaves the stage.)

7 Life in the Young Republic

Objectives

- Determine biographical facts about a number of United States presidents.
- Study the main achievements and notable elements of each presidency.
- Create a biographical cereal box based on the information gathered.

Quest Collaborative Discussion: Presidential Cereal Box

	Description	Duration	Materials	Participants
STEP 1 Set the Stage	Read two blackline masters as an introduction to the project.	15 minutes	**Blackline Master:** Quest Kick Off, **Blackline Master:** Executive Letter	Whole Class
STEP 2 Launch the Activities	Assign a president to each group.	5 minutes	**Leveled Readers:** The First U.S. Presidents; The Early Presidents of the United States; Defining the Presidency: Our Nation's First Presidents	Small Groups
Activity 1 Presidential Portraits	Create the cover art for the cereal box using a portrait of a president.	20 minutes	Classroom or Library Media Center resources, art supplies (optional); model unmodified cereal box (optional)	Small Groups
Activity 2 Back to Basics	Describe and illustrate two notable elements of a presidency.	35 minutes	Classroom or Library Media Center resources, various art supplies; model unmodified cereal box (optional)	Small Groups
Activity 3 Fun Facts	Create a list of facts unrelated to the presidency about each president.	20 minutes	Classroom or Library Media Center resources, paper cut into strips which fit the width of the type of cereal box the students will be using, model unmodified cereal box (optional)	Small Groups
Activity 4 By the Numbers	Create a side panel of the box with mostly numerical facts about a president.	20 minutes	**Blackline Master:** By the Numbers, classroom or Library Media Center resources	Small Groups
Activity 5 Advertising Jingle	Write an advertising jingle for the cereal.	15 minutes		Small Groups

STEP 3 Complete the Quest Complete Your Cereal Boxes	Assemble information on cereal boxes.	20 minutes	Completed Quest materials, empty cereal boxes (either teacher-provided or student-provided), various art supplies; scissors; glue or glue sticks; craft paper or newsprint (optional)	Small Groups
Deliver a Presentation **ELL**	Present cereal boxes to the panel of reviewers and host a discussion.	45 minutes		Small Groups
Answer the **Compelling Question**	Discuss the compelling question.	15 minutes		Whole Class

Quick Activities

	Description	Duration	Materials	Participants
The Trail of Tears	Draw the routes for the Trail of Tears on a map.	20 minutes	**Blackline Master:** Mapping the Trail of Tears, **Video:** Cherokee Heritage Center: A Trail of Tears, classroom or Library Media Center resources	Partners
The Great Irish Famine ELL	View an illustration depicting the poverty during the famine and have a group discussion.	15 minutes	**Primary Source:** Miss Kennedy Distributing Clothing at Kilrish	Small Groups
Lewis and Clark Expedition	View and answer questions about a map of Lewis and Clark's journey.	20 minutes	**Blackline Master:** Lewis and Clark Expedition **Student Activity Mat:** 1A United States	Individual
Star Spangled Banner	Discuss, listen to, and study the lyrics of the U.S. national anthem.	15 minutes	**Blackline Master:** National Anthem; Recorded rendition of "The Star Spangled Banner"	Whole Class
Readers Theater: Larger Than Life: Paul Bunyan	Perform a brief skit about the legend of Paul Bunyan.	30 minutes	Script	Small Groups

Collaborative Discussion: Presidential Cereal Box

 Compelling Question **What are the qualities that make a good leader?**

Welcome to Quest 7, Presidential Cereal Box. In this Quest, your students will be studying the lives of early United States presidents, creating an informational cereal box, and engaging in a civic discussion. Their study of the lives of the presidents will prepare them to discuss the compelling question at the end of this inquiry.

Objectives

- Determine biographical facts about a number of United States presidents.
- Study the main achievements and notable elements of each presidency.
- Create a biographical cereal box based on the information gathered.

STEP 1 Set the Stage ⏱15 minutes

Begin the Quest by distributing the blackline master **Quest Kick Off.** It will bring the world of the Quest to life, introducing a story to interest students and a mission to motivate them.

Story

The makers of the fictional cereal "Executive Crunchies" are celebrating the one-year anniversary of their flagship product. They want to design "special edition" boxes of cereal featuring a series of early United States presidents.

··

Mission

Your students are a design team hired to help the makers of Executive Crunchies design their presidential-themed cereal boxes.

STEP 2 Launch the Activities

The following five activities will help students prepare for their presentation by researching the lives of the presidents and creating an informational cereal box.

Divide students into small groups that will remain consistent for all the activities. Assign one of the following United States presidents to each group:

- George Washington
- John Adams
- Thomas Jefferson
- James Madison
- Andrew Jackson

Distribute the blackline master **Executive Letter,** which further explains the mission. You may assign the appropriate Leveled Reader for this chapter.

Activity 1 **Presidential Portraits** (20) minutes

Materials: Classroom or Library Media Center resources, art supplies (optional); model unmodified cereal box (optional)

Explain to students that to design the front cover of their cereal boxes, they must find a portrait of and a few important dates concerning their assigned president.

Have students use classroom or Library Media Center resources to find a portrait of their president. The following Web site may be helpful:

https://www.whitehouse.gov/photos-and-video/photogallery/official-portraits-us-presidents

Students may copy or print out a portrait found online, or if desired, draw a picture of the president based on one of these portraits. Remind students that their portraits will need to be large enough to feature prominently on a cereal box. Once this has been done, students should look up the dates of the assigned president's life and presidency, and write them in place of the weight measurement section on a cereal box (pass around the example cereal box for reference if desired). Have the students write the dates of the presidency, with the dates of the president's life inside parenthesis.

Students should also draw a bowl of cereal to be featured with the picture of the president. This can be done on a separate sheet of paper if the students want to create an "overlap" effect on the finished box.

Activity 2 — Back to Basics — 35 minutes

Materials: Classroom or Library Media Center resources, various art supplies; model unmodified cereal box (optional)

Using the model cereal box if desired, explain to students that the backs of their cereal boxes should explain two things that their president is most known for during their presidency (e.g., George Washington determined the role of the cabinet, or Thomas Jefferson bought the Louisiana Purchase).

Have students use classroom or Library Media Center resources to determine the two main facts that they want to list. Then have the groups work to create two separate paragraphs, each one explaining one of the facts. Have the students draw pictures to illustrate each. Remind students to list important names and dates within their paragraphs if warranted.

Activity 3 — Fun Facts — 20 minutes

Materials: Classroom or Library Media Center resources, paper cut into strips which fit the width of the type of cereal box the students will be using, model unmodified cereal box (optional)

Using the model cereal box if desired, explain to students that the side panel of a cereal box can be used to list additional information about the cereal. Explain that in this case, the side panel will be dedicated to listing a series of "Fun Facts" about each president which are unrelated or tangential to their presidency (e.g., the apocryphal story of George Washington and the cherry tree, or the fact that Thomas Jefferson and John Adams died within hours of each other on July 4, 1826). Hand out the strips of paper.

Have the students use classroom or Library Media Center resources to determine the facts that they might list. As they research, remind students that the facts need to fit on the strips of paper that were handed out in order to fit along the side of the box. Encourage students to include information about the presidents' personal lives, personality quirks, or any number of short, interesting pieces of information.

Activity 4   By the Numbers   20 minutes

Materials: Blackline Master: By the Numbers, classroom or Library Media
Center resources, model unmodified cereal box (optional)

Using the model cereal box to illustrate if desired, explain to the students that
in this activity, they will be creating a set of primarily numerical facts about their
presidents which will take the place of the "Nutrition Facts" section of a cereal box.

Distribute the blackline master **By the Numbers,** which provides a set space for
students to input certain data about their assigned president.

Have the students conduct the necessary research using classroom or Library
Media Center resources to fill out the worksheet. Explain that they will cut out the
needed section of their worksheets when they assemble the cereal boxes.

Activity 5   Advertising Jingle   15 minutes

Explain to students that in order to make an advertising jingle, or short song,
they can use a very simple musical theme (such as the first two bars of "Twinkle,
Twinkle Little Star," or "Mary Had a Little Lamb") and set new lyrics to it that talk
about the cereal. Remind students that the song should feature information about
their assigned presidents.

Have students write down their lyrics and what tune they should be sung to.
Encourage the students to use humor and rhyming in their jingle.

STEP 3   Complete the *Quest*

Part 1   Complete Your Cereal Boxes   20 minutes

Materials: Completed Quest materials; empty cereal boxes (either teacher-provided
or student-provided), various art supplies; scissors; tape, glue, or glue
sticks; craft paper or newsprint (optional)

Using empty cereal boxes, students will begin to affix their drawings and information
to the respective parts of the box. If desired, boxes can be covered with craft paper
or newsprint beforehand in order to let students start with a neutral surface.

Be sure that students include all of the information that they have gathered.
Encourage them to decorate the box further and add details that make the box
visually appealing.

Part 2 Deliver a Presentation 45 minutes

Set up the classroom so that the groups are in a large circle, facing inwards. Have each group display their cereal boxes, and, if possible, have a number of faculty members present to function as a panel of reviewers from Executive Crunchies. If there are visitors present, explain the nature of the inquiry, and hand out the **Quest Kick Off** and the **Executive Letter** blackline masters from the beginning of the Quest. The groups will take turns presenting their cereal boxes to the panel, describing each side, and end by singing their jingle. When the presentations are complete, the audience members should be encouraged to circulate to view the boxes and ask questions of the group members if desired. The class should then host a collaborative discussion about the presidents that were studied. Encourage students to ask specific questions about the leadership qualities of the presidents studied by other groups, and to answer the questions posed by other students. To complete the discussion, have the students offer their conclusions about the successes and challenges of the early United States presidency.

ELL Support for English Language Learners

Writing: Explain to students that a successful presentation is one that is organized and well thought out. Tell students that this activity will help them to organize their cereal box presentations to give them a more formal and professional feel.

Entering: Have students look at their cereal boxes. Point to the front and label it "1." Then help students determine where they want a user to go to next, a side or the back? Help students understand that they want to make sure they talk through the information in the right order so that the person looking at it knows where to go.

Emerging: Have students look at their cereal boxes. Explain that since they are presenting the cereal box to the panel of reviewers, they should begin by saying who the cereal box represents, and they should present the front of the box with the portrait of the president. Have each student list three things that they can say about the front cover of their cereal boxes during the activity.

Developing: Have students study the information they have on their cereal boxes and decide the order they want to present the information. Suggest that the front is the most logical place to start. Then ask pairs of students to list one or two facts that they want to share about each side.

Expanding: With their cereal boxes in front of them, explain to students that they will need to present the parts of the box in a certain order. Explain that they should start by explaining the front of the box, since it contains the introductory information about their president. Explain to students that they can determine the order in which they present the remaining information. Have students list the order in which they will present the sides of their cereal box, and have them write down two points that they will make about each side.

Bridging: Have students look at their cereal boxes. Explain that they will need to determine the order in which to present the information on the various sides of the box. Have students determine the order and create an outline listing three points that they plan to make about each side of their cereal box. Provide assistance as necessary.

Part 3 Compelling Question minutes

After students finish presenting their cereal boxes, encourage them to reflect on what they learned. As a class, discuss the compelling question for this Quest "What are the qualities that make a good leader?"

Students have learned about the lives and legacies of early United States presidents. Encourage students to think about the qualities present in the lives of each of these presidents. They should use what they learned to answer the compelling question.

PRESIDENTIAL
CEREAL BOX

The makers of the fictional cereal "Executive Crunchies" want to celebrate their one-year anniversary by making a series of cereals featuring some of the early American presidents. They need help designing cereal boxes that will help people learn about the presidents that they want to feature.

Your Mission

Your design team has been hired by the makers of "Executive Crunchies" to research and design a cereal box featuring one of the early United States presidents.

To help you to design your cereal box, work with your team to do the following:

Activity 1 Presidential Portraits: Design the front of the cereal box, using the portrait of the assigned president.

Activity 2 Back to Basics: Describe and illustrate two things which make the assigned presidency notable.

Activity 3 Fun Facts: Create a side panel for the cereal boxes listing fun facts about the president but that are unrelated to the office of the presidency.

Activity 4 By the Numbers: Research to find a set of numerical information about the assigned president.

Activity 5 Advertising Jingle: Write a short advertising jingle, using a simple tune.

Complete Your Quest

Present your cereal boxes to the panel of Executive Crunchies reviewers and discuss the presidents.

Executive Letter

To the Design Team:

Here at Executive Crunchies, Inc., we strive to provide our customers with the very best in breakfast enjoyment. In just a few months, we will be celebrating our one-year anniversary. In honor of this, we hope to release a series of presidential-themed cereals which will not only nourish the body, but will nourish the mind.

In light of this, we would like your team to design a cereal box packed full of information about one of the following five presidents:

- George Washington
- John Adams
- Thomas Jefferson
- James Madison
- Andrew Jackson

We will need not only *information* for the box design, but *artwork*. Please make all artwork on-topic and engaging; we want our customers to be delighted by our designs. This box should be a feast for the eyes!

Thank you for your kind attention to this matter. We will review your submissions once they are complete.

Sincerely,

Arthur Cruncherton

Fictional CEO of Executive Crunchies, Inc.

P.S. Please also write a jingle that we can use for an advertisement.

By the Numbers

Fill in the information about your assigned president of the United States below. Cut out and affix to the side panel of your cereal box.

Date of birth:

_____

Dates of presidency:

_____

Ordinal (first, second, third president):

_____

Number of terms served:

_____

Other political offices held:

_____

Spouse name (if any):

_____

Number of children:

_____

Lived here after presidency:

_____

Date of death:

_____

Quick Activities

The Trail of Tears

Materials: Blackline Master: Mapping the Trail of Tears, Video: Cherokee Heritage Center: A Trail of Tears, classroom or Library Media Center resources

Begin by showing the video **Cherokee Heritage Center: A Trail of Tears,** which will give students the content background they need to complete the activity.

Explain to the class that in order to allow white settlers to claim land in the southeastern United States, President Andrew Jackson signed the Indian Removal Act in to law on May 28, 1830. Explain that this law was the beginning of a process which ultimately led to the forced relocation of the Cherokee, Muscogee, Seminole, Chickasaw, and Choctaw Indians. Part of this forced relocation occurred during the winter of 1838–1839, and the harsh conditions led to disease and death amongst the Indian nations. Explain that the brutal nature of the journey combined with the high mortality rate led to the removal effort being known as the "Trail of Tears."

Distribute the blackline master **Mapping the Trail of Tears,** which shows a map of the area in which the Indian nations were led on their way to be relocated in what is now Oklahoma.

Have students read the handout. Then have pairs of students use classroom or Library Media Center resources to find the routes used in the forced relocation effort known as the "Trail of Tears," and draw them in the map. Students should be able to locate at least one route. For context, explain that the journey was approximately 1,000 miles long, and that the length of this journey (which many American Indians travelled by foot) is nearly as long as a journey up the entire California coastline, which is about 1,100 miles long.

The Great Irish Famine

Small Groups (15) minutes

Materials: Primary Source: Miss Kennedy Distributing Clothing at Kilrish

Remind students that one of the primary motivators for immigration to the United States has historically been to seek more economic opportunity. Explain that in the case of the Great Irish Famine (also known as the "Potato Famine"), Irish immigrants were attempting to escape not only economic disadvantage but starvation. The journey had hazards of its own, however; many people died along the way due to diseases that spread in crowded conditions and to malnourishment.

Distribute the blackline master **Primary Source: Miss Kennedy Distributing Clothing at Kilrish** which shows the dire condition of many of the Irish. Have students study the handout and answer the critical thinking question. Then divide students into small groups, and have them imagine that they are a family living in Ireland at the time of the famine. Have them discuss the advantages and disadvantages of emigrating to the United States, and decide whether or not to risk the journey. Then have each group explain their decision and reasons.

· ·

ⓔ Support for English Language Learners

Speaking: Explain that students will need to be able to express their opinions and give reasons for them in order to make a convincing case for their point. Distribute blackline master **Primary Source: Miss Kennedy Distributing Clothing at Kilrish.**

Entering: Read the handout with students and discuss the image. Ask students to share what they see in the image and what they think it means. Have pairs of students record a reason to stay in Ireland and a reason to emigrate.

Emerging: Have students look at the handout in pairs. Have each student state one reason for leaving Ireland due to the famine, and explain why. Then have students work together to come up with one good reason to stay in Ireland.

Developing: Have students read the handout and discuss the image. Then help students list two to three reasons for leaving Ireland and one to two reasons for staying. You may need to help students think of some of the issues with leaving a place. Remind students to use their lists in their group discussion.

Expanding: Have students study the handout and think of three reasons for leaving Ireland and three reasons for staying. Have the groups discuss why each of these reasons is good, and explain to students that they can use this information to back up their opinions during the activity.

Bridging: Have students review the handout and come up with three reasons for staying in Ireland or three reasons for leaving. Explain that understanding the objections to our positions can help us to more readily back up our opinions. Have students write responses to each of these reasons, arguing from the other point of view.

Lewis and Clark Expedition

Individual minutes

Materials: Blackline Master: Lewis and Clark Expedition, **Student Activity Mat:** 1A United States

Be sure that students understand that before 1803, the land west of the Mississippi was not controlled by the United States, but rather by other European countries, and that a large block was owned by France. Explain that in 1803, French Emperor Napoleon Bonaparte sold this land to the United States. President Thomas Jefferson then commissioned a team of volunteers to explore the territory. Share **Student Activity Mat:** 1A United States with students. Point out the area east of the Mississippi River and the area that was not part of the United States. Have students label which country controlled each territory.

Distribute the blackline master **Lewis and Clark Expedition,** which shows a map of the United States with the routes that Lewis and Clark took. Have students read the handout and answer the questions. Circulate to provide assistance as needed.

Star Spangled Banner

Whole Class 15 minutes

Materials: Blackline Master: National Anthem; recorded rendition of "The Star Spangled Banner"

Introduce students to the concept of a "national anthem." Explain that the United States national anthem, "The Star Spangled Banner," began as a poem written by Francis Scott Key after a battle during the War of 1812. Having watched a British attack on Fort McHenry and seen the American flag flying the morning after the unsuccessful onslaught, he was inspired to write a poem which he set to the tune of a popular song. This song ultimately became the United States national anthem.

Distribute the blackline master **National Anthem,** which shows the lyrics of the United States national anthem.

Have students review the handout. Quickly go through any difficult vocabulary as a class, and then play a rendition of the national anthem while students follow the lyrics on the handout.

If desired and if time permits, encourage students to memorize the lyrics and have volunteers recite the lyrics as a poem, using appropriate rate and cadence. Have the class discuss the difference between reciting the lyrics and singing them.

Name _____ Date _____

Mapping the Trail of Tears

As land-hungry U.S. settlers expanded into the Southeast, they wanted to take over the land that had long been held by the Cherokee, Muscogee, Seminole, Chickasaw, and Choctaw. In 1830, President Andrew Jackson signed the Indian Removal Act into law. The act allowed the President to make treaties, or agreements, with Indian groups living east of the Mississippi River which would force the Indians to give up their lands in exchange for lands in the West.

Some Indian groups signed treaties and some did not. Whether or not they signed, all Indians were forced off their lands and sent to "Indian Territory" which is today the state of Oklahoma. The harsh conditions of this forced relocation of approximately 100,000 people caused much suffering and many deaths. The brutal conditions caused the relocation to be called the "Trail of Tears."

Use the resources that your teacher provides to research the Trail of Tears. Then on the map below, draw some of the routes taken by Indian nations during the forced relocation.

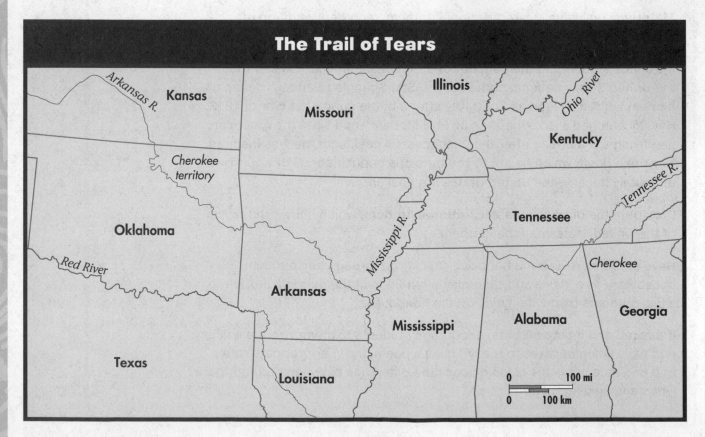

The Trail of Tears

Miss Kennedy Distributing Clothing at Kilrish, 1849

This is a drawing of Miss Kennedy, a wealthy young girl of around seven years old. She is giving away clothing to the poor of Ireland during the time of the Great Irish Famine. Notice that she is dressed warmly and well, while the people surrounding her are wearing rags. Study the drawing and the facts below, and fill in the short answer.

Facts:
- Potatoes were the staple crop of the Irish poor, since they were nutritious and easy to grow.

- When a potato disease called "blight" ruined an enormous portion of the potato crop in 1845, widespread famine caused the death of nearly one million people. Another one million fled to other countries.

1. Imagine that you are the editor of a newspaper featuring this image. Using your study of the image and the facts listed, write a sentence or two telling your readers about the Great Irish Famine.

_____

_____

Lewis and Clark Expedition

In May of 1804, William Clark and Meriwether Lewis set out to explore the land the United States had gained from France in the Louisiana Purchase. Study this map of their journey, and answer the questions below.

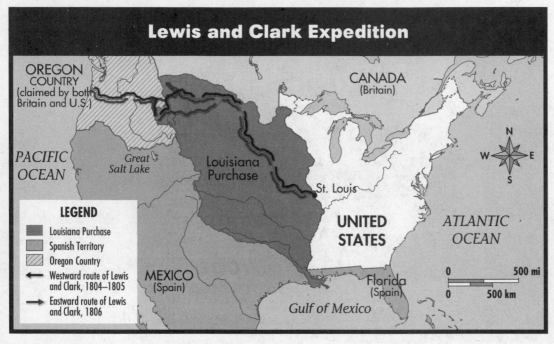

1. Using the map's scale, can you tell approximately how many miles Lewis and Clark traveled?

_____

2. Where did the expedition begin?

_____

3. Describe the furthest point west that Lewis and Clark reached using points of reference on the map.

_____

Fun Facts

Lewis and Clark's journey took more than two years. Today, a commercial jet can travel the same distance in about eight hours.

National Anthem

These are the lyrics to the United States' national anthem, "The Star Spangled Banner," by Francis Scott Key. Ask your teacher to define any words that you do not understand, then follow along as you listen to the anthem.

O say can you see, by the dawn's early light,

What so proudly we hailed at the twilight's last gleaming,

Whose broad stripes and bright stars through the perilous fight,

O'er the ramparts we watched, were so gallantly streaming?

And the rockets' red glare, the bombs bursting in air,

Gave proof through the night that our flag was still there;

O say does that star-spangled banner yet wave

O'er the land of the free and the home of the brave?

Larger Than Life: Paul Bunyan

Irish immigrant children hear the story of Paul Bunyan for the first time.

The Parts

5 players:

- **Bridget**, young Irish immigrant
- **John**, young Irish immigrant
- **Michael**, young Irish immigrant
- **Old Joe**, a mischievous storyteller
- **Mama**, the childrens' mother

Director's Notes:

Some children are playing while their mother is cooking breakfast for them inside. They are immigrants, and together they had previously walked down into the Boston area from Canada through Maine. The children are pretending they are building a house in the Maine woods. Old Joe is sitting on his porch nearby and overhears them and tells them a story of Paul Bunyan, who was born in the Maine woods.

Bridget: Okay, so now that we've found a good place for our log cabin, we need to cut down trees to build it! Do you have your ax?

John: Yes, I do...but you chop too, it will take too long to build a house if I'm the only one chopping!

Michael: Okay, so let's chop! Chop the trees! Knock them down and make a clearing, let's go!

Old Joe:
who has been watching them with a smile on his face
Hello there—building a house, are ye? Old Joe, by the way, nice to meet you all.

Bridget: Nice to meet you Mr. Joe, and yes, sir—we're building a house in the Maine woods.

Old Joe: Ah, the Maine woods! Well, it'll take ye a mighty long time to get a house going there—that is, unless you have Paul Bunyan helping you. Then you'll get it done in a jiffy.

John: Paul who?

Old Joe: Paul Bunyan. Why, he could be chopping trees with one hand while he was building your house with his other!

Bridget: He could?

Old Joe: Maybe you could too if you were almost as tall as a pine tree yourself. Why, Paul can comb his beard with a pine tree! Paul Bunyan is the greatest lumberjack in the world!

John: But nobody can do that!

Bridget: And nobody could ever be that big.

Michael:
turning aside and whispering to the others
Well, nobody where *we* come from. But how do we know there's no such thing in America? Those woods were bigger than we had ever seen. Maybe there's a lumberjack bigger than we've ever seen.

Old Joe: Paul was even big when he was a baby. Why, he was wearing his father's clothes in his first week of life! He was knocking down trees at the age of two, took after his father. Really helped with the family logging business.

Bridget: Nobody could do that as a baby!

Old Joe: Nobody but Paul. Why, have you heard of the Grand Canyon out in Arizona?

John:	Yes, we've heard of it. Mama says it's enormous!
Old Joe:	Well, just how do you think it *got* that way?
John:	I think it's from the river, isn't it? Did Paul go there?
Old Joe:	A river! Why, that canyon was formed when Paul dropped his ax off his shoulder and let it drag behind him because of the desert heat!
Bridget:	I don't think this is possible…
Mama:	Children! Breakfast in five minutes, get ready to come inside!
Michael:	Oh, good! Breakfast time. I'm hungry, and I think Mama's making flapjacks.
Old Joe:	Flapjacks, eh? Paul Bunyan ate flapjacks for breakfast too, except he needed to eat so many that his cooks couldn't keep up, and they were getting frantic. So he made a griddle the size of a skating rink, and the cooks greased it up by tying bacon slabs to their feet and skating on it.
Michael:	Mr. Joe? Is this a true story? I mean, how could anyone do those kinds of things?
Old Joe: *winking at the children with a mischievous look on his face*	Well, let's just say that here in America, we like our tales as tall as our lumberjacks.
John:	I don't underst….

Mama:	Come on in, children!
Bridget:	Coming Mama! It was nice to meet you, Mr. Joe. When we're done with breakfast, can you tell us more about Paul Bunyan?
Old Joe:	Surely will. I'll tell you the story of his big blue ox, Babe, who Paul found in a snowdrift.
Bridget:	Wow, thank you!
John: *turning to the others*	Do you think the story is true?
Michael:	I'm not sure. But if there are more stories like that about America from Mr. Joe, I think I'm going to like it here!

8 Westward Expansion

Objectives

- Examine the circumstances around a variety of historical events and innovations.
- Describe various aspects of life from the point of view of a fictional historical character.
- Recognize points of view through reading other historical journal entries.

Quest Project-Based Learning: My Historical Journal

	Description	Duration	Materials	Participants
STEP 1 Set the Stage	Read a blackline master to introduce the project.	15 minutes	**Blackline Master:** Quest Kick Off	Whole Class
STEP 2 Launch the Activities	Divide students into small groups and distribute informational blackline masters.	10 minutes	**Fact Sheets:** Factory Work; 1800s Transportation; The Alamo; Moving West; Gold Rush **Leveled Readers:** A Changing Nation; The Growth of America; America at the Turn of the 19th Century	Small Groups
Activity 1 My Journal	Write an introductory journal entry.	30 minutes	**Fact Sheets,** classroom or Library Media Center resources (optional); crayons, markers, or colored pencils	Small Groups
Activity 2 ELL "Today Was So Exciting..."	Describe an exciting event.	20 minutes	**Fact Sheets,** classroom or Library Media Center resources (optional)	Small Groups
Activity 3 An Ordinary Day	Describe an ordinary day.	20 minutes	**Fact Sheets, Student Activity Mat:** 3A Graphic Organizer classroom or Library Media Center resources (optional)	Small Groups
Activity 4 "Today Was Awful..."	Describe an unfortunate event.	20 minutes	**Fact Sheets, Student Activity Mat:** 3A Graphic Organizer classroom or Library Media Center resources (optional)	Small Groups
Activity 5 Wrap It Up	Write an entry evaluating each experience.	25 minutes	**Fact Sheets,** classroom or Library Media Center resources (optional)	Small Groups
STEP 3 Complete the Quest Share Completed Journals	Share and read classroom journals.	45 minutes	Journal Entries from Quest Activities 1–5, **Fact Sheets**	Whole Class

Answer the Compelling **Question**	Discuss the compelling question.	⏱ 15 minutes		Whole Class

Quick Activities

	Description	Duration	Materials	Participants
California Song	Write lyrics about California's statehood to a favorite tune.	⏱ 20 minutes	**Blackline Master:** California Statehood Lyrics Sheet	Small Groups
Comparing Points of View ELL	Compare two quotes from persons who lived in the 1800s.	⏱ 20 minutes	**Blackline Master:** Comparing Sources: Laura Ingalls Wilder and Luther Standing Bear	Whole Class
Pony Express	View an ad for the Pony Express and write an essay about communication.	⏱ 25 minutes	**Blackline Master:** Pony Express Ad **Student Activity Mat:** 1A United States	Individual
Readers Theater: Along the Oregon Trail, 1850	Perform a brief skit about a family on the Oregon Trail.	⏱ 30 minutes	Script	Small Groups

Project-Based Learning: My Historical Diary

 **Compelling Question** ## What were the costs and benefits of life in the 1800s?

Welcome to Quest 8, My Historical Diary. In this Quest, students will be writing a series of journal entries from the perspective of various people from the 1800s. Their study of the circumstances under which people from the nineteenth century lived will enable them to discuss the compelling question at the end of this inquiry.

Objectives

- Examine the circumstances around a variety of historical events and innovations.
- Describe various aspects of life from the point of view of a fictional historical character.
- Recognize points of view through reading other historical journal entries.

STEP 1 Set the Stage ⏱15 minutes

Begin the Quest by distributing the blackline master **Quest Kick Off.** It will bring the world of the Quest to life, introducing a story to interest students and a mission to motivate them.

Story

The fictional nineteenth century magazine *The Westward Gazette* is looking to include a serial feature detailing the experiences of a "modern" young person. The editors have sent out an invitation to young people living in and around the United States to submit their journal entries.

....

Mission

Create a series of journal entries for submission to the magazine from the perspective of a young person from the 1800s.

STEP 2 Launch the Activities

The following five activities will help students complete their journal by directing them to write from the perspective of their character in a variety of different scenarios. Note that all five can be done independently of the larger Quest. You may assign the appropriate Leveled Reader for this chapter.

Divide students into five small groups that will remain consistent for all the activities. Assign each group one of the persons in the following scenarios and hand out the appropriate **Fact Sheets:**

- Child of immigrants working in a factory
- Young person witnessing a new mode of transportation (steamboat or railroad)
- Young American or Tejano (native of Mexico) in Texas during the Battle of the Alamo
- Child of parents who decide to move west and travel in a wagon train
- Young person who decides to move to California during the gold rush and witnesses California becoming a state

---

Activity 1 My Journal   minutes

Materials: Fact Sheets; classroom or Library Media Center resources; crayons, markers, or colored pencils

Explain to students that in order to begin their historical journal, they need to create an introductory entry that briefly explains who they are, and what their circumstances are. Tell students that in writing their first entries, they should imagine that their assigned characters are beginning a journal for the first time, so students should write from that point of view.

Distribute the appropriate **Fact Sheets** to each group. They provide background information for each of the scenarios.

Explain to students that they will use their fact sheets to help them to understand the circumstances of their character. Direct them to additional classroom or Library Media Center resources as needed. Remind students to include their character's name, along with information about their character's family, location, and circumstances.

Encourage students to draw a picture of their character, noting the kinds of clothing that their character would wear.

Materials: Fact Sheets, classroom or Library Media Center resources (optional)

In this activity, students will write a journal entry that details something exciting from their character's scenario.

Distribute the appropriate **Fact Sheets,** which provide background information for each scenario.

Explain to students that their characters should write about something exciting (e.g., the students to whom the gold rush was assigned might write about striking gold). Encourage students to include as many details as they can, and to have their character express any thoughts or feelings that may come to mind as a result of the excitement (happy, nervous, etc.). Provide classroom or Library Media Center resources. Remind students to date their entry.

🄴🄻🄻 Support for English Language Learners

Writing: Explain to students that in writing their journal entries, they are describing events and how their character feels about the events. Writing about an event requires a sequential narrative, while writing about ideas, opinions, or feelings requires the writer to refer back to the original idea.

Entering: Write these sentences on the board: *I twisted my ankle. I can't go to dance class. I am sad..* Explain that the order of these sentences can change because the sentences all focus on a single idea. Then write these sentences on the board: *I went to the pool. I met my friends. We had fun swimming.* Discuss how these sentences are sequential. Discuss how students need to use different writing styles for their journals.

Emerging: On the board, write three sequential sentences and discuss the order of the events. Next, write the sentence *My bike broke.* Write three sentences stemming from this original idea (e.g., *I felt upset, I couldn't get around as well, I have to save up to buy a new one.*) Explain that in the second example, the sentences focus around an idea. Discuss different scenarios and type of writing needed.

Developing: Ask students to tell a simple story about some event (e.g., how we gathered for the class assembly, or how we go to lunch at school). Write each sentence on the board in a sequence. Next, have the students describe something simple that they like. Write what they describe, using a main idea model. Explain that model is useful when talking about opinions, arguments, or feelings. Have pairs take turn telling events in different styles.

Expanding: Tell a simple story to students that requires sequential writing and write it on the board using arrows to show the progression. Then tell a story about something you like. Write this story on the board using a main idea model. Explain to students that they will need these models to write their journals.

Bridging: Discuss with students how writing sequentially is different then writing about ideas. Then have pairs of students work together to write two sample journal entries. One entry should be written sequentially and the other should be written about a main idea and supporting details.

Activity 3 **An Ordinary Day** (20) minutes

Materials: Fact Sheets, **Student Activity Mat:** 3A Graphic Organizer,
classroom or Library Media Center resources (optional)

Students will write an entry that helps to provide deeper context for their
character's experience.

Distribute the appropriate **Fact Sheets,** which provide background information
for each scenario. You may want to share the **Student Activity Mat:** 3A Graphic
Organizer so that students can record information about their character as they
read the fact sheet.

Explain that this entry should include details about what ordinary life is like for
their character. Students may choose to write about the foods their character eats,
day-to-day living conditions, and the kinds of people their character encounters.
Provide classroom and Library Media Center resources as desired. Remind
students to consult their fact sheets, and to date their entries.

Activity 4 **"Today Was Awful..."** (20) minutes

Materials: Fact Sheets, **Student Activity Mat:** 3A Graphic Organizer,
classroom or Library Media Center resources (optional)

This entry will deal with a negative event that happens in each character's life.

Distribute the appropriate **Fact Sheets,** which provide background information
for each scenario. You may want to share the **Student Activity Mat:** 3Λ Graphic
Organizer so that students can record information about their character as they
read the fact sheet.

Explain that each scenario features various negative elements. Instruct students
to consult their fact sheets, and select an unfortunate event that they will detail
from their character's point of view. Tell students that this event could involve
the character directly, the character's family, or someone in the character's
community. The entry should include the character's thoughts and feelings about
the event, as well as any material effect that the event might have on the character
(in the case of injury, death, loss of work, etc., of a providing family member). If
desired, allow students to consult classroom or Library Media Center resources.
Remind students to date their entries.

Activity 5 Wrap It Up (25) minutes

Materials: Fact Sheets, classroom or Library Media Center
resources (optional)

Students should use this entry to summarize the experience of their character, and to give "final thoughts" that the character has about his or her circumstances.

Distribute the appropriate **Fact Sheets,** which provide background information for each scenario.

Ask students to think about the experiences of their character, and to imagine how their character would feel about what has gone on. Have students write an entry summing up their feelings about the situation they are in. Have these "final thoughts" include whether the character is ultimately happy or unhappy with the choices that have been made (technological, immigratory, political, and so on.) Remind students to date their entries.

STEP 3 Complete the *Quest*

Part 1 Display Your Journals (45) minutes

Materials: Journal Entries from Quest Activities 1–5,
Fact Sheets

Have each group take turns reading the first entry of their historical journals aloud. Then have each group set up a station in the classroom. Some members of each group should stay at the station to answer questions, while the other group members circulate to read the other groups' entries. Have students switch halfway through so that every student has a chance to read the journals. Be sure that each group displays the **Fact Sheet** for their character's situation at the station.

Part 2 Compelling Question (15) minutes

After students finish reading all of the journal entries, encourage them to reflect on what they learned. As a class, discuss the compelling question for this Quest "What were the costs and benefits of life in the 1800s?"

Students have learned about many different scenarios that people found themselves in during the 1800s. They should think about how these scenarios would have affected the point of view of the people in question. They should use what they learned to answer the compelling question.

My Historical Journal

The new fictional nineteenth-century magazine the *Westward Gazette* is looking to run a series of journal entries written from the perspective of a young person from the 1800s. They want to show what life is like during this time period for people in and around the expanding United States.

Your Mission

Create a series of journal entries to submit to the editors of the *Westward Gazette* from the perspective of a fictional person living in the 1800s, using your assigned scenario as a guide.

To prepare your historical diary:

Activity 1 **My Journal:** Create an introductory journal entry, and draw a picture of the character you are portraying.

Activity 2 **"Today Was So Exciting..."** Write an entry that explains something exciting that happened in your assigned scenario.

Activity 3 **An Ordinary Day:** Write an entry that explains some of the details in your character's day-to-day life.

Activity 4 **"Today Was Awful..."** Write about a negative or sad event that your character experienced.

Activity 5 **Wrap It Up:** Wrap up by writing a final entry.

Complete Your Quest

Display your historical journal. Then read the journals of the other groups to learn more about life in the 1800s.

Name _____ Date _____

Factory Work

Before the early nineteenth century, most goods (such as cloth or guns) were made by hand, a long, labor-intensive process that required skilled workers. However, in 1798, Eli Whitney (already known for the invention of the cotton gin) revolutionized the manufacturing industry with the concept of "interchangeable parts," which sped up the production of goods. It also did not require the use of skilled labor in factories, so more people qualified for jobs.

Factories were often unpleasant and dangerous places to work. The new technology provided speed, but not safety. Deaths were not uncommon, and workers were often injured on the job, sometimes in ways that would permanently affect their ability to work. Workers were often expected to work more than 70 hours per week. Factories were usually very loud and hot, with poor air quality. Children were also often employed under these extreme conditions, since there were no laws against child labor at the time.

Immigrants were often given the most dangerous jobs, and for the least amount of pay. Since they had often come to America to escape poverty, immigrants relied on their jobs to feed and support themselves and their families. Some immigrants faced cultural and language barriers, and employers often took advantage of their situation and paid them less.

Cities became more crowded as many people moved there to find permanent work. Disease spread more easily in the crowded conditions, and many people became ill and died.

1800s Transportation

In the early 1800s, transportation options were limited. People walked and relied on horsepower to move over land, and boats or rafts could be used for water transport.

River currents made it possible for large loads to travel downstream, but upstream travel was difficult, since boats had to rely on wind power or manual force to work against the current. With the use of steam power, however, practical two-way river travel became possible, and the early nineteenth century saw the first steamboats come into use. In 1807, the *Clermont* made its first public voyage up the Hudson River, bringing a new age of transportation technology. The boats relied on a steam engine to run a paddlewheel, which provided enough power for the steamboat to move against a current.

The same technology that made steamboats possible also allowed for easier land travel. Railroads using steam locomotives made it easier and faster to travel by land than ever before. By the 1870s, railroads stretched across the entire continental United States and had become the primary means of long-distance transportation. Early trains ran their engines by burning coal, which created large plumes of smoke, and caused workers and passengers alike to be covered in soot. Train travel was improved with the widespread use of the telegraph in the 1850s, which allowed train operators to coordinate train schedules and helped to prevent accidents.

Name _____ Date _____

The Alamo

In 1821, the nation of Mexico won its independence from Spain, which had previously controlled Mexico as a colony. At that time, Texas was a province of Mexico. To encourage an increase in its population, Mexico passed laws that granted land to anyone willing to colonize. Many United States citizens settled in the province of Mexican Texas, which bordered the southern United States.

Colonists in the Texas province began to be dissatisfied with the Mexican government. In turn, the Mexican government began to distrust the American colonists. In 1835, fighting broke out between the (primarily American) colonists and the Mexican government. Shortly after, Texans formed a separate government.

The President of Mexico, Antonio López de Santa Anna, was angry and did not want to lose Texas, so he led an army of several thousand soldiers to a former Franciscan mission, the Alamo, which the Texan soldiers were using as a fort. The Texan soldiers had been asking the Texas government for supplies and for additional troops, but they had received very few. The Texan army, which consisted mostly of volunteers (including the famous American frontiersman and congressman Davy Crockett), found itself surrounded by Mexican troops on February 23, 1836.

The Texan army refused to surrender. The Mexican army had marched a long distance without enough food and in bad weather, and the Mexican soldiers were weakened as a result. The Texans fought off the Mexican army for 13 days. When the Mexican army advanced on the fort on the morning of March 6, 1836, the nearly 200 men who fought to defend the Alamo all died, along with more than 1500 Mexican troops.

Moving West

After William Clark and Meriwether Lewis made their famous journey to the Pacific Northwest, many other Americans began to make their way west, mostly to gain land. The farmland of Oregon particularly was said to be very fertile, and by 1843 many families were leaving their homes for the West.

The four- to six-month trip west required many supplies and much preparation, and only the most necessary items could be brought. Families packed everything they could into large wagons covered with waterproofed cotton cloth called prairie schooners, which were pulled by oxen. The settlers would say goodbye to their families and friends in the east, knowing that they might never see them again.

People usually traveled in groups, called wagon trains, and hired a guide to lead them to their intended destination. Traveling in large numbers was safer, as a group of settlers was less likely to be a target for thieves and could help one another along the way. The trip had to be timed carefully. Leaving too early meant that the grass had not grown enough to meet the needs of the hungry oxen, and leaving too late meant that the travelers risked traveling in winter, which was dangerous and often deadly.

Many people died along the trail. The wagon was mostly for supplies, and people had to be strong to walk the long distances without much shelter. Accidents, diseases, and starvation were all risks. Conflicts with American Indians, who lived on the land prior to the settlers, could also lead to death. Animals could die too, and would-be settlers were sometimes stranded when too many of their animals died, leaving them unable to continue the journey.

Gold Rush

When James Marshall discovered gold at Sutter's Mill in California in January of 1848, it set off a flurry of excitement across the United States, and even across the world.

Mexico had only just recently ceded control of the California Territory to the United States when news about the discovery of gold in California began spreading across the United States. A huge number of gold seekers, nicknamed "49ers" for the year in which most came, filled the territory with prospectors looking to mine gold. Most of these were United States citizens, but immigrants from South America and China were common, too.

Unlike many settlers who came west with their families to claim land, most prospectors, or people searching for gold, were single men. These men often lived in tents and did their own cooking. Beans, bacon, and sourdough bread were some of the main components of the miners' diets. Some even brought their sourdough starters (a doughy mixture of flour, water, and wild yeast) with them as they traveled, and California remains famous for its sourdough bread.

While at the beginning of the gold rush some miners could make up to $2,000 per day (about $50,000 in today's money), it was more common to make around $10 (about $300). Because prices for food and supplies were so high, this was sometimes not enough to pay for living expenses. Many miners were poorly nourished because of this.

Gold gradually became harder to find as more of it was mined, and by about 1855, the gold rush was over. However, the dramatic population boom helped speed up California's application for statehood, and it was admitted to the Union in September 1850.

Quick Activities

California Song

Materials: Blackline Master: California Statehood Lyrics Sheet

Start by reviewing some of the facts of California's statehood with the students. Explain that the United States obtained the territory that is now California in the Treaty of Hidalgo. Remind students that the gold rush brought many immigrants to California in a relatively short period of time. Explain that this population boom was one of the reasons that California's petition for statehood, started in 1849, went through so quickly and led to California's admission to the Union in 1850.

Distribute the blackline master **California Statehood Lyrics Sheet,** which shows the California state flag and provides space for writing song lyrics.

Explain to students that California has a state song called "I Love You California." Have students imagine that they have been called upon to write another state song for California, using the tune from one of their favorite appropriate popular songs. In small groups, have students work together to rewrite the lyrics of an agreed-upon song to reflect facts about California's statehood as related in the class discussion. When complete, have each group perform their new song in front of the class.

Comparing Points of View

Materials: Blackline Master: Comparing Sources: Laura Ingalls Wilder and Luther Standing Bear

Explain to students that westward expansion of American citizens was largely viewed differently by settlers and by American Indian nations. Tell students that settlers and American Indians often found themselves at odds with one another over attitudes toward land.

Distribute the blackline master **Comparing Sources: Laura Ingalls Wilder and Luther Standing Bear,** which shows a quote from each famous author.

Have students read the two quotes. Ask students to volunteer what they think each author's viewpoint about land is. Discuss the differing points of view, and how they led to conflict. Explain that many settlers wanted to own and farm land that traditionally belonged to Indian nations. Encourage students to be vocal and to participate in the class discussion.

· ·

🅔🅛🅛 Support for English Language Learners

Reading: Explain to students that this activity requires reading two quotes carefully to determine their meanings, and how they are different. Distribute the blackline master **Comparing Sources: Laura Ingalls Wilder and Luther Standing Bear.**

Entering: Read each quote on the handout out loud. Be sure students understand the quotes. Have students work in small groups to determine the main idea of each quote. Help students contrast and compare the quotes.

Emerging: Read each quote out loud to students. Then separate the class into two groups, and have each group determine the main idea of one of the quotes. Provide support as needed, writing out and defining any words that students do not know. Explain to students that these ways of viewing land are different. Explain to students that they will use this information to compare and contrast the two quotes in the activity.

Developing: Read the handout with students. Make sure they understand each quote. Discuss the different points of view represented by each quote. Have groups of students write one to two sentences that explain each point of view. Tell students that they can use these statements to help compare and contrast the quotes.

Expanding: Have students take turns reading the quotes on the handout (line by line) in small groups. Have the groups determine the way land is viewed in each of the two quotes. Provide support as needed. Have each group explain the view of land from each of the quotes to the class. Help students see how the two quotes give contrasting views as to the nature of land.

Bridging: Have students read the quotes to themselves and write out the main idea of each. Remind them to focus on the way land is viewed in each. When students have finished writing the main idea, ask them to note the differences in the viewpoints.

Pony Express

Individual (25) **minutes**

Materials: Blackline Master: Pony Express Ad, **Student Activity Mat:**
1A United States

Remind students that in the early 1800s, land-based transportation relied
heavily on horsepower. Explain that as more settlers began moving west,
the United States needed a form of reliable communication between
settlers and their families back home. Explain that a service called the
Pony Express aimed to meet the need for speedy and reliable mail delivery.

Distribute the blackline master **Pony Express Ad,** which shows an
advertisement for the Pony Express mail service from 1861. Share the
Student Activity Mat: 1A United States with students. Have them find
New York and San Francisco and explain that it is over 3,000 miles.

Have students review the handout. Point out how long it took for a letter
to reach San Francisco from New York. Explain that this was considered
a very short time during this time period, and that the service operated
by having a rider go as quickly as he could with the mail until the next
stop, where he was either relieved by another rider or given a fresh horse
so that he could continue on. Have students note that this ad advertised
a speedy form of existing communication, and use the example of a
modern-day ad advertising faster Internet speeds.

Ask students to write a short essay describing what they think is the
fastest and most reliable form of communication today. Students may
decide on e-mail, texting, phone calls, or other social or traditional
media. Have them back up their opinions with reasons why they chose
that form of communication. Be sure that students end their opinion
piece with an appropriate concluding statement.

California Statehood Lyrics Sheet

Write out the lyrics for a new "State of California" song using what you have learned about California's statehood. Then color the flag.

CALIFORNIA REPUBLIC

To the tune of _____

_____

_____

_____

_____

_____

_____

_____

_____

_____

Comparing Sources: Laura Ingalls Wilder and Luther Standing Bear

Laura Ingalls Wilder is an author made famous by her autobiographical account of life as a pioneer in the 1800s. Luther Standing Bear is a Lakota Indian who was educated in a white-run boarding school and wrote about his nation in English. Read the two quotes from the two famous authors and answer the questions.

> "This country goes three thousand miles west, now. It goes' way out beyond Kansas, and beyond the Great American Desert, over mountains bigger than these mountains, and down to the Pacific Ocean. It's the biggest country in the world, and it was farmers who took all that country and made it America, son. Don't you ever forget that."
> –Laura Ingalls Wilder, *Farmer Boy*, 1933

> "The American Indian is of the soil, whether it be the region of forests, plains, **pueblos,** or **mesas.** He fits into the landscape, for the hand that fashioned the continent also **fashioned** the man for his surroundings. He once grew as naturally as the wild sunflowers, he belongs just as the buffalo belonged . . ."
> –Luther Standing Bear, Oglala Sioux, *Land of the Spotted Eagle*, 1933

Vocabulary

pueblo, *n.,* a settlement of Indians, especially in the American southwest, characterized by multistory adobe houses

mesa, *n.,* an isolated flat-topped hill with steep sides

fashion, *v.,* to make

1. Based on the text selection, how do you think that each author would define "America"?

2. How does each author seem to view land, and how do these views conflict?

Pony Express Ad

The Pony Express was a mail service that connected California with the eastern United States by offering speedy and reliable mail delivery. Riders were expected to ride at top speed day and night. Then they would quickly pass their mail to the next rider, who would do the same until the mail reached its destination. Study the following ad for the Pony Express.

Along the Oregon Trail, 1850

A story about a family on the Oregon Trail.

The Parts

4 players:

- **Daniel Haywood,** father
- **Mary Haywood,** mother
- **Jonathan Haywood,** son
- **Abraham Haywood,** son

Director's Notes:

The Haywood family, a group of pioneers on the Oregon Trail, is gathered around the campfire after a long day. They are discussing their life and family back home in the east.

Daniel:	Well everyone, we've reached the two-month mark today. Two months ago, we left Independence, Missouri. If everything goes well from here, we're halfway done.
Jonathan:	Has it been that long?
Abraham:	I think it seems like longer.
Daniel:	Think of it—six hundred twenty beautiful acres of farmland, ours for just showing up.
Mary:	That really is a lot. I can hardly believe they are giving it away for free.
Daniel:	They want the place settled up! And nothing gets people moving like free land.
Jonathan:	I know that's a lot of land . . . but I liked our old farm. I still miss it.
Mary:	I miss it too, honey. And I miss Aunt Jane and Uncle Peter, and the twins, and Grandma, too. But we can write letters to them, and who knows? Maybe when they hear our stories of how wonderful it is, they'll also want to head to Oregon.

Abraham: Well, we'd better not tell them *some* of the stories from our trip.

Jonathan: Yes, I don't think they'll want to come as much if they hear how three families came down with that sickness where they had that terrible fever and couldn't keep any food down, what was it? Oh yes, dysentery . . . and two people died from it.

Abraham: I don't think Aunt Jane would want to come yet anyway. The twins are really little for a long trip like this.

Jonathan: I've seen a lot of little children, maybe even younger than the twins, running around. Isn't Mary Scott only two?

Daniel: I think so, and Virginia Tiller even had a baby while we were on the road, remember?

Mary: I surely do. We stopped the wagon train for a whole day. And I finally got some washing done, I remember. Not always a lot of time for it otherwise.

Abraham: Aunt Jane hates being wet, though, remember? I don't think she'd like it having to walk along in the rain. She got really angry when we set that bucket of water up to spill on her head.

Daniel:
winking
Well good grief, who wouldn't have been? Though I admit, it was a clever trick how you set the bucket up just right, and that look on her face . . .

Mary:
hiding a laugh
Dan!

Daniel: It's true though that Jane and Peter like living in a town. A shopkeeper like Peter can live a more clean and comfortable life than farmers like us.

Abraham: I heard Aunt Jane tell Ma that she didn't want to leave her furniture behind, and she didn't understand how Ma could do it.

Mary: Well, we can't have everything. Pa can make us some new furniture when we get to Oregon and set up our claim. Right, Dan?

Daniel:	You bet. And maybe even buy some, once we get going with the farm.
Jonathan:	But some people tried to bring furniture, didn't they, Pa? Didn't the Hendersons bring chairs in their wagon?
Daniel:	They did. And good luck to them! They might make it all the way—but from what I've heard, most folks end up leaving all of that heavy stuff along the side of the road when they have to cross rivers or when their oxen are tired. The oxen are strong, but they can't pull forever. And if folks don't take care of their oxen, what will happen?
Abraham:	They'll end up stuck!
Daniel:	Exactly.
Jonathan:	Are our oxen healthy?
Daniel:	They are. They're good and strong, and we packed as light as we could to ease the load on them. They're good animals.
Jonathan:	What do people do when they're stranded, Pa?
Daniel:	Well, they can usually stay put with their supplies for awhile until somebody comes along to be able to help them out.
Jonathan:	I don't want to be stranded.
Daniel:	Well like I said, our oxen are nice and healthy, and I aim to keep it that way.
Abraham:	Would that happen to Aunt Jane and Uncle Peter if they tried to bring all of their furniture?
Daniel:	I don't think Aunt Jane and Uncle Peter will be finding out.
Abraham:	Will we never see them again, then?

Daniel:	Well, I don't think they'll ever come in a covered wagon with an eye toward moving. But let me tell you something—I'm guessing that before long, the railroad companies are going to build a train that goes straightway across this nation. Mark my words, there'll be a train that connects the East and the West. When that happens, we can visit anyone we like, and they can visit us.
Jonathan:	We should have waited for the train, Pa!
Abraham:	I want to ride a train to Oregon!
Mary: *smiling*	Well right now we're riding a prairie schooner to Oregon, and the sky is looking an awful lot like bedtime.
Abraham:	Already?
Daniel:	You heard your Ma. Off with you both. Goodnight, boys.
Jonathan and Abraham:	Goodnight, Ma. Goodnight, Pa.

Objectives

- Study the background of the conflict between the North and the South prior to the Civil War.
- Analyze the early documents of the United States.
- Defend a position supporting or opposing the possibility of secession in a civic discussion.

Quest Collaborative Discussion: To Secede or Not to Secede				
	Description	**Duration**	**Materials**	**Participants**
STEP 1 Set the Stage	Read a blackline master as an introduction to the project.	15 minutes	**Blackline Master:** Quest Kick Off	Whole Class
STEP 2 Launch the Activities	Watch a video with background information.	5 minutes	**Video:** Gettysburg National Battlefield: Fighting for a Cause **Leveled Readers:** Freedom!; Journeys to Freedom; Pathways to Freedom	Whole Class
Activity 1 A Nation Divided	View a map and information about slave and free states.	20 minutes	**Blackline Master:** A Nation Divided: A Map of North and South in 1860 **Student Activity Mat:** 1B United States Outline	Small Groups
Activity 2 Establishing Intent	Analyze an excerpt from the Declaration and identify what each part supports.	25 minutes	**Primary Source:** Establishing Intent: From the Declaration, Venn Diagram graphic organizer	Small Groups
Activity 3 Conventions From the Constitution	Read an excerpt from the Constitution and answer questions as a group.	20 minutes	**Primary Source:** Conventions From the U.S. Constitution	Small Groups
Activity 4 The First State Leaves the Union	Review South Carolina's declaration of secession and questions.	20 minutes	**Primary Source:** South Carolina Leaves the Union: Declaration of Secession	Small Groups
STEP 3 ELL Complete the Quest Discuss Your Findings	Discuss your findings to prepare to defend a position.	30 minutes	Quest Materials	Small Groups

	Description	Duration	Materials	Participants
Hold a Collaborative Discussion	Discuss the basis of the positions taken by the North and the South.	45 minutes		Whole Class
Answer the **Compelling Question**	Discuss the compelling question.	15 minutes		Whole Class

Quick Activities

	Description	Duration	Materials	Participants
Civil War Postage Stamp	Design a postage stamp of a Civil War–era person.	20 minutes	Poster board, art supplies, classroom or Library Media Center resources, postage stamps or pictures of postage stamps (optional)	Small Groups
Letter to the Editor	Write an opinion letter about whether the war was worth fighting.	20 minutes	Classroom or Library Media Center resources **Student Activity Mat:** 3A Graphic Organizer	Individuals
Reconstruction Matching Game	Play a matching game using terms about Reconstruction.	15 minutes	Index cards	Partners
Songs of the Civil War	Review and compare two songs from the time of the Civil War.	15 minutes	**Primary Source:** "The Bonnie Blue Flag," **Primary Source:** "The Battle Cry of Freedom," classroom or Library Media Center resources	Whole Class
Civil War Crossword **ELL**	Complete a crossword using Civil War terms.	15 minutes	**Blackline Master:** Civil War Crossword, classroom or Library Media Center resources	Partners
Readers Theater: A House Divided	Perform a brief skit about a family during the Civil War.	30 minutes	Script	Small Groups

Collaborative Discussion: To Secede or Not to Secede

QCompelling**Question**

What does it mean for a state or country to be free?

Welcome to Quest 9, To Secede or Not to Secede. In this Quest, your students will study important documents from the early United States. Their study of these documents will enable them to participate in a collaborative discussion about how both the Union and the Confederacy justified their actions during the Civil War. This study will also enable them to discuss the compelling question at the end of this inquiry.

Objectives

- Study the background of the conflict between the North and the South prior to the Civil War.
- Analyze the early documents of the United States.
- Defend a position supporting or opposing the possibility of secession in a civic discussion.

STEP 1   Set the Stage   ⏱ minutes

Begin the Quest by distributing the blackline master **Quest Kick Off.** It will bring the world of the Quest to life, introducing a story to interest students and a mission to motivate them.

Story

The fictional country of Democritas has laws very similar to those of the United States. They are wondering whether they should amend their constitution to address the possibility of secession by one of their states. They have hired a team of researchers to study important documents from the founding of the United States.

· ·

Mission

Students have been hired by the governing body of Democritas to study the issue of secession using early United States documents. They will then hold a civic discussion to determine whether the Southern states had a legal and ideological basis for seceding from the Union.

STEP 2 Launch the Activities

The following four activities will help students prepare for their civic discussion by giving them the information that they need to defend the position of either the North or the South.

Begin by showing the chapter video **Gettysburg National Battlefield: Fighting for a Cause,** which will give students some of the content background they need to complete the activities. You may also assign the appropriate Leveled Reader for this chapter. Then divide students into an even number of small groups that will remain consistent for all the activities.

Activity 1 A Nation Divided 20 minutes

Materials: Blackline Master: A Nation Divided: A Map of North and South in 1860, **Student Activity Mat 1B** United States Outline (optional)

Explain that by 1804 the Northern states had banned the practice of slavery, while the South continued it.

Distribute the blackline master **A Nation Divided: A Map of North and South in 1860** which shows a map of the United States as it was in 1860. You may want to use **Student Activity Mat 1B** United States Outline to have students fill in the states in the North and the South with different colors.

Have students look at the map and study the list of facts. In their small groups, have the students discuss why the Southern states may have wanted slavery to be allowed in new states admitted to the Union. Ask what they think might have happened if there were more free states than slave states. Then have volunteers share their answers with the class.

Activity 2 Establishing Intent 25 minutes

Materials: Primary Source: Establishing Intent: From the Declaration, Venn Diagram graphic organizer

Remind students that the first document of the newly formed United States was the Declaration of Independence.

Distribute the blackline master **Primary Source: Establishing Intent: From the Declaration**, which shows an excerpt from the Declaration of Independence divided into three sentences, each of which addresses a different concept.

Have students read from the handout. Then distribute the Venn Diagram graphic organizer. Ask the students to label one of the circles "North" and the other "South." Have the students determine which of the three sentences the North might have used to justify its position, which sentence(s) the South might have used, and any sentence(s) they might have both agreed upon. Have them write the corresponding letter of the sentence in the diagram. Then review the diagrams as a class.

Activity 3 **Conventions From the Constitution** 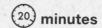 minutes

Materials: Primary Source: Conventions From the U.S. Constitution

Remind students that the Constitution is the "law of the land," and that every other law in the United States is derived from or compatible with what is written in the Constitution.

Distribute the blackline master **Primary Source: Conventions From the U.S. Constitution**, which shows an excerpt from the Constitution relating to the admission of new states into the Union.

Have the students review the excerpt. In their small groups, have students work to answer the two questions on the handout. Have the groups read their answers to the class, and discuss.

Activity 4 **The First State Leaves the Union**  minutes

Materials: Primary Source: South Carolina Leaves the Union: Declaration of Secession

Explain to students that shortly after the election of President Lincoln (who believed slavery was immoral, and wanted to see it limited in new states), South Carolina became the first state to formally secede from the nation.

Distribute the blackline master **Primary Source: South Carolina Leaves the Union: Declaration of Secession,** which shows an excerpt from the document declaring South Carolina's separation from the Union.

Have students read the handout. Provide assistance with understanding if required. Then have students discuss the following questions in their small groups:

• Is this document more similar to the Declaration of Independence or the Constitution? Why?

• Based on what you have read from the documents of the early United States, do you think this document is justified? Why or why not?

Circulate as needed to provide support and answer questions. If desired, review the groups' answers as a class.

STEP 3 Complete the Quest

Part 1 Discuss Your Findings ⏱ 30 minutes

Materials: Quest materials

Explain to students that they will be preparing for their civic discussion. Assign each small group to defend either the North's position (that the Union cannot be broken up) and the South's position (that states have a right to secede when they do not feel represented). Have the groups meet together to discuss the evidence. Be sure they have access to all of the prior Quest materials. Each group should plan how they intend to present the evidence in order to be convincing.

ⓔ Support for English Language Learners

Reading and Speaking Provide students with the Quest materials.

Entering: Have each student work with a partner to identify one sentence in the Quest materials that supports their assigned side.

Emerging: Have students identify one sentence in the Quest materials that supports their assigned side. Have them read the sentence out loud.

Developing: Divide students into small groups. Ask each group to find one sentence from the Quest materials that supports the North's position and one that supports the South's position. Have each student say why the sentences support the positions.

Expanding: Direct each student to identify two sentences in the Quest materials that support the position opposite theirs. Have the students explain why the sentences support the other side.

Bridging: Have each student identify a sentence that supports the position that is opposite theirs. Then have them explain how they will respond to the sentence to defend their position.

Part 2 Hold a Civic Discussion ⟨45⟩ minutes

If desired, invite another class or faculty members to listen in on the discussion. Provide copies of the Quest materials to all in attendance. Have the two sides sit opposite one another in the classroom, and discuss whether the North's position or the South's position was the correct one, given the documents they have read. Use the following questions to help guide the discussion:

- What are the most basic American values, according to the early documents of the United States?
- What role does unity play in the formation of a country?
- How might the threat of secession affect how the government is run?
- The Declaration of Independence was written as a response to British rule, where the colonists did not have any say in government. Was this the case with the South, as South Carolina's secession declaration implied? Why or why not?
- What are some risks of a central government that can overrule the states?
- One of the hallmarks of the Constitution is the balance between federal government and state government. Based on what you have read, which do you think should be stronger?

Be conscious of letting both sides speak on each question. If desired and if time permits, visitors can be allowed to ask questions of the group.

Part 3 Compelling Question ⟨15⟩ minutes

After students complete the civic discussion, encourage them to reflect on what they learned. As a class, discuss the compelling question for this Quest "What does it mean for a state or country to be free?"

Students have learned about why the Union and the Confederacy believed they were following American values. Encourage students to think about what each side was defending. They should use what they learned to answer the compelling question.

To Secede or Not to Secede

The fictional country of Democritas has a problem. They need to know if they should amend their constitution to address the possibility of secession. Since their laws are similar to the laws of the United States, they have hired a team of researchers to study the early documents of the United States to see whether those documents support the case for the South's secession from the Union.

> **Your Mission**
> Research early United States documents, and participate in a discussion about which early U.S. documents better support the position of the North or the South.

To prepare for your discussion:

Activity 1 **A Nation Divided:** View a map showing slave states and free states.

Activity 2 **Establishing Intent:** Study an excerpt from the Declaration of Independence.

Activity 3 **Conventions From the Constitution:** Examine an excerpt from the Constitution.

Activity 4 **The First State Leaves the Union:** Study an excerpt from South Carolina's official statement of secession.

Complete Your Quest

Hold a civic discussion concerning whether the South had or should have had the right to secede from the Union.

A Nation Divided: A Map of North and South in 1860

The United States in 1860 was growing larger, but was also growing apart. Slavery was one of the dividing issues between the North and South. This map shows the division between free states and slave states in 1860.

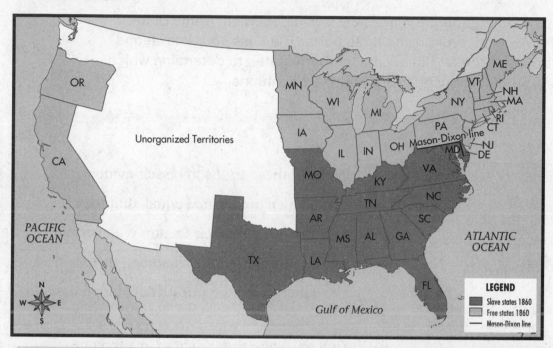

Path to Conflict

- **Missouri Compromise, 1820:** When Missouri petitioned for statehood, Congress argued over whether new states should be able to allow slavery. Eventually, a compromise was reached: Missouri would be admitted as a slave state, while Maine would enter as a free state. The Mason-Dixon line was established as a guide: new states above the line would be free, new states below would allow slavery.

- **Compromise of 1850:** As the battle over slavery continued, Congress came up with new compromises for states wanting to enter the Union. One result was the Fugitive Slave Act, which required that any enslaved persons captured in the North must be returned to their Southern owners. Previously, once an enslaved person had escaped to the North, they were considered free.

- **Dred Scott Case, 1857:** Dred Scott was an enslaved man whose owner had brought him to live in a Northern state where slavery was illegal. When Scott petitioned the court for his freedom, the Supreme Court ruled that because he was not a citizen, he had no legal standing and would not be freed. This decision was very unpopular in the North.

🔍 Primary Source

Establishing Intent: From the Declaration

The Declaration of Independence is the most basic document of the United States. Read this excerpt, broken into three parts. Then use your knowledge of the conflict between the Northern and Southern states to determine which statements they might have used to support their positions.

Vocabulary

endowed, *v.,* given as a gift

unalienable, *adj.,* not able to be removed

pursuit, *n.,* search

instituted, *v.,* put in place

deriving, *v.,* getting

abolish, *v.,* do away with

institute, *v.,* form

effect, *v.,* cause to make happen

A. We hold these truths to be self-evident, that all men are created equal, that they are **endowed** by their Creator with certain **unalienable** Rights, that among these are Life, Liberty and the **pursuit** of Happiness.

B. That to secure these rights, Governments are **instituted** among Men, **deriving** their just powers from the consent of the governed.

C. That whenever any Form of Government becomes destructive of these ends, it is the Right of the People to alter or to **abolish** it, and to **institute** a new Government, laying its foundation on such principles and organizing its powers in such form, as to them shall seem most likely to **effect** their Safety and Happiness.

Activity 3

🔍 Primary Source

Conventions From the U.S. Constitution

Read this excerpt from the United States Constitution. Then answer the questions.

New States may be **admitted** by the Congress into this Union; but no new State shall be formed or erected within the **Jurisdiction** of any other State; nor any State be formed by the **Junction** of two or more States, or Parts of States, without the Consent of the Legislatures of the States concerned as well as of the Congress. The Congress shall have Power to **dispose** of and make all needful Rules and Regulations respecting the Territory or other Property belonging to the United States; and nothing in this Constitution shall be so **construed** as to **Prejudice** any Claims of the United States, or of any particular State.

Vocabulary

admitted, *v.*, allowed into

jurisdiction, *v.*, area of legal authority

junction, *v.*, joining

dispose, *v.*, remove

construed, *v.*, made to look like

prejudice, *v.*, exist prior or in contrast to

How does this passage relate to the conflict between the North and the South?

_____

_____

How does it relate to the excerpt from the Declaration of Independence?

_____

_____

🔍 Primary Source

South Carolina Leaves the Union: Declaration of Secession

South Carolina was the first state to secede from the Union. In a document entitled "Declaration of the Immediate Causes Which Induce and Justify the Secession of South Carolina from the Federal Union," the state gave the reasons for its secession.

In the year 1765, that portion of the British Empire **embracing** Great Britain, **undertook** to make laws for the government of that portion **composed** of the thirteen American Colonies. A struggle for the right of self-government **ensued**, which resulted, on the 4th of July, 1776, in a Declaration, by the Colonies, "that they are, and of right ought to be, FREE AND INDEPENDENT STATES; and that, as free and independent States, they have full power to **levy** war, conclude peace, contract alliances, establish **commerce**, and to do all other acts and things which independent States may of right do.

We, therefore, the People of South Carolina . . . have solemnly declared that the Union **heretofore** existing between this State and the other States of North America, is **dissolved**, and that the State of South Carolina has resumed her position among the nations of the world, as a separate and independent State . . .

Vocabulary

embracing, *v.,* taking as one's own

undertook, *v.,* began as a project

composed, *v.,* made up of

ensued, *v.,* began

levy, *v.,* impose, bring about

commerce, *n.,* business dealings

heretofore, *adv.,* until this point

dissolved, *v.,* broken up

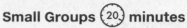

Civil War Postage Stamp

Materials: Poster board, art supplies, classroom or Library Media Center resources, postage stamps or pictures of postage stamps (optional)

Explain that one way that the United States celebrates famous people or events is by putting their image on a postage stamp. If desired, pass around examples of postage stamps or pictures of postage stamps. Then divide students into small groups, and give each group a piece of poster board and art supplies. Assign each group one of the following people from the time of the Civil War: **Frederick Douglass, Robert E. Lee, Harriet Beecher Stowe, Clara Barton, Jefferson Davis,** or **Abraham Lincoln.**

Explain that students will be creating their own postage stamp featuring their assigned person. Encourage students to use classroom or Library Media Center resources to find out what kind of imagery to use on their stamps along with the pictures of their assigned persons. Remind students that they should come up with a new and original design.

Finally have each group explain the connection their assigned person has to the Civil War, and how the images they chose relate to their assigned person.

Letter to the Editor

Materials: Classroom or Library Media Center resources, **Student Activity Mat** 3A Graphic Organizer (optional)

Have students imagine that they are living at the time of the Civil War, and that the editor of a local newspaper asks people to write to the paper with their opinions of whether the war is worth fighting. Randomly assign each student one of the following characters:

- Confederate woman whose husband is a soldier
- African American Union soldier
- Battlefield doctor

Provide classroom and Library Media Center resources so that students can look up what life might have been like for their assigned characters. You may want to use **Student Activity Mat** 3A Graphic Organizer to help students organize their research. Then have the students write an opinion letter to the editor of the newspaper from their character's point of view, describing whether or not they think the war is worth fighting. Remind students to use specific examples from their assigned character's life and circumstances to support their opinion.

Reconstruction Matching Game

Partners (15) **minutes**

Materials: Index cards

Explain that students will be preparing a matching game, using terms relevant to the time of reunification of the North and the South known as Reconstruction.

Hand out index cards, and have students work with a partner to write the following, with the term on one card and the definition on another (read aloud or write on the board):

- **The Thirteenth Amendment** made slavery illegal in the United States.
- **President Lincoln** began a plan for rebuilding the South called Reconstruction.
- **President Johnson** fought with Congress so much over Reconstruction that Congress tried to impeach him.
- **The Fourteenth Amendment** gave the rights of citizenship and equal protection under the law to formerly enslaved persons.
- **The Fifteenth Amendment** gave all male citizens the right to vote.
- **Black codes** were laws designed to make it difficult or impossible for freed African Americans to vote or hold certain types of jobs.
- **Segregation** is the practice of separating people, usually by race.

Then have students turn all the cards facedown, and mix them up. Have partners take turns turning over two cards to see if they can match the Reconstruction term with its definition. Play continues until all cards are matched.

Songs of the Civil War

Whole Class (15) **minutes**

Materials: Primary Source: "The Bonnie Blue Flag," Primary Source: "The Battle Cry of Freedom"

Explain that music has often been a part of military operations, and that both the Union and the Confederacy had songs meant to heighten morale and reaffirm the principles of their respective causes.

Distribute the blackline masters **Primary Source: "The Bonnie Blue Flag"** and **Primary Source: "The Battle Cry of Freedom,"** which show the lyrics to two popular Civil War–era songs.

Have students review the lyrics, or read them aloud as a class. Then ask the following questions:

- What is the significance of the flag in each of the songs?
- Do you notice anything similar about how the songs are structured?
- What can you infer about the values of the Union and the Confederacy from the lyrics to these songs?

If desired, students can listen to the songs being performed. The 2003 movie *Gods and Generals* has a rendition of "The Bonnie Blue Flag," and the following Web site features a performance of "The Battle Cry of Freedom": https://www.civilwar.org/learn/primary-sources/civil-war-music-battle-cry-freedom.

Civil War Crossword

Partners ⏱ 15 minutes

Materials: Blackline Master: Civil War Crossword, classroom or Library Media Center resources

Review the basics of crossword puzzles with students, including the use of clues and the difference between vertical and horizontal orientation of words.

Distribute the blackline master **Civil War Crossword**, which is a crossword puzzle using vocabulary terms related to the Civil War.

Have students work with a partner to complete the crossword puzzle using the clues on the handout. Provide classroom or Library Media Center resources as needed for the students to reference. When students have completed the crossword, review the answers as a class.

🔵 Support for English Language Learners

Writing: Distribute the blackline master **Civil War Crossword**.

Entering: Have students work in small groups. Assign each group one of the clues for the crossword, and have the group determine which vocabulary word matches the clue.

Emerging: Divide students into pairs and assign each pair three clues. Have the partners write complete sentences using the clues and vocabulary words.

Developing: In small groups, assign one of the vocabulary words to the group. Have the group members work together to write their own explanation of the word.

Expanding: Have each student select one of the vocabulary words from the handout. Then have the students write what the word means using their own words.

Bridging: Instruct students to select one vocabulary word from the handout. Have each student write a short paragraph using the word in its correct historical context.

The Bonnie Blue Flag

In the early days of the Confederacy, there was no official flag. Different military units would design and fly their own flags for marching into battle. One of the earlier flag designs was the "Bonnie Blue Flag," which was a battle flag flown during the battle of Fort Sumter. These are the lyrics to a song named after this flag that was popular with Confederate soldiers.

We are a band of brothers And native to the soil, Fighting for the property We gained by honest toil; And when our rights were threatened, The cry rose near and far— "Hurrah for the Bonnie Blue Flag That bears a single star!"

CHORUS:

Hurrah! Hurrah! For Southern rights hurrah! Hurrah for the Bonnie Blue Flag That bears a single star.

As long as the Union Was faithful to her trust, Like friends and like brothers Both kind were we and just; But now, when Northern treachery Attempts our rights to mar, We hoist on high the Bonnie Blue Flag That bears a single star.

CHORUS

The Battle Cry of Freedom

Since the American Revolution, the United States flag has been a symbol of freedom and unity. Although the Southern states had begun to declare their separation from the Union in 1860, the Union did not recognize this separation and the flag continued to sport thirty-three stars; one for each state. These lyrics, which reference the Union flag, belong to a song that was popular with Union soldiers during the Civil War.

Yes, we'll rally round the flag, boys, We'll rally once again, Shouting the battle cry of Freedom, We will rally from the hillside, We'll gather from the plain, Shouting the battle cry of Freedom.

CHORUS:
The Union forever, Hurrah! boys, hurrah! Down with the traitors, Up with the stars; While we rally round the flag, boys, Rally once again, Shouting the battle cry of Freedom.

We are springing to the call Of our brothers gone before, Shouting the battle cry of Freedom; And we'll fill our vacant ranks with A million free men more, Shouting the battle cry of Freedom.

CHORUS

We will welcome to our numbers The loyal, true and brave, Shouting the battle cry of Freedom; And although they may be poor, Not a man shall be a slave, Shouting the battle cry of Freedom.

Civil War Crossword

Use the clues to fill in the crossword with the words from the list of terms provided.

abolitionist	Reconstruction
secede	assassination
Union	amendment
Confederacy	sharecropper
emancipation	impeach

Across

2. The freeing of slaves is called _____.

4. South Carolina was the first state to _____ from the Union.

6. Congress tried to _____ President Johnson.

7. An _____ believed that slavery should be made illegal.

8. The Northern states were referred to as the _____.

Down

1. The Southern states referred to themselves as the _____.

3. John Wilkes Booth played a primary role in the _____ of President Lincoln.

5. A _____ used a portion of the harvest to pay the rent for the land.

7. Each change to the Constitution requires an _____.

9. _____ is the effort undertaken by the United States government after the Civil War to rebuild the South.

Civil War Crossword

A story of a family forced to confront their differences during the start of the American Civil War.

The Parts

4 players:

- **Thomas Wordsworth**, a young man
- **Margaret Wordsworth**, the mother of Thomas, William and Samuel
- **William Wordsworth**, a young man
- **Samuel Wordsworth**, a young boy

Director's Notes:

A family from Virginia is sitting around a table. Margaret is knitting, William is reading a book, and Samuel is playing nearby. Thomas comes in and everyone looks at him; they can tell that something is wrong. Margaret stands up. Samuel watches with wide eyes.

Thomas:	Mother, I think you had better sit down.
Margaret: *putting her hand to her mouth*	Thomas, no . . .
Thomas:	I've enlisted, Mother. And it isn't with the Confederacy.
Margaret: *hiding her eyes*	Thomas, how could you? Your father will be so ashamed . . . what in the world am I going to tell him?
Thomas: *shrugging*	The truth, what else? Tell him that I'm a Union boy now.
William: *leaping up*	A Union boy! For shame, Thomas. Father's been fighting for the Confederacy all this time, and I'm to join him soon. What will he say to one of his own sons betraying his heritage?
Thomas:	Heritage? Don't we all come from the same heritage? A state cannot just declare itself separated, we are one country, united! We cannot be narrow-minded . . .

Margaret:
scowling

Narrow-minded indeed! Your father has owned this plantation for generations. His father's father fought in the Revolution! We fought then for our rights to determine our own way and seize hold of our own happiness! And what does the Union have to do with us anymore? They've been trying to take away our ways, and what do they know of our traditions?

Thomas:

Mother, we cannot just abandon our country.

Margaret:

Enough! William, talk some sense into him. I declare, I'm shaking like a leaf. I'm going to lie down.

Margaret storms off. William approaches Thomas. Samuel keeps watching with wide eyes.

William:

Thomas . . . are you really quite sure? What of our right to self-determination, our right to be free?

Thomas:

No one is taking away *your* right to be free.

William:

The North doesn't understand us, Thomas! And now they've gone and elected Lincoln, and you know how he feels about slavery. Why, if we lost our slaves we'd be ruined!

Thomas:

You know how *I* feel about slavery. But even apart from that. You think you can just leave your country when it doesn't suit you?

William:

The Union betrayed us! No one wants to enforce the Fugitive Slave Act, they don't want our slaves returned to us.

Thomas:

Do you know how much courage and character it takes to go North, what with the search parties always on the lookout? If someone makes it up there, they deserve to be free. Your problem is that you don't want freedom for everyone.

William:
looking uncomfortable
Samuel walks over to them.

I . . .

Samuel:

William?

William:

Yes, Samuel?

Samuel:

If we were slaves, would we go to the North?

William:

What do you mean?

Samuel:

I mean, do you think we'd be brave enough to go to the North if we were slaves? To be free?

Everyone pauses. Samuel looks around, confused.

Thomas:

From the mouths of babes, William. Well, what's your answer? Would you go to the North?

Margaret:
calling from offstage

William? Have you talked him out of it yet?

William:

No, Mother.

Thomas:

Well, I have to pack a bag. I'm wanted tomorrow morning, and who knows how long I'll have to march.

William:
reaching his hand out to him

Take . . . take care of yourself. And . . . I hope I don't meet you. On the battlefield, I mean.

Thomas:
giving him a firm handshake

I hope so too.

Samuel:

Where are you going, Thomas?

Thomas:
grinning, and pausing a moment for effect

North!

Name _____ Date _____

K-W-L Chart

What We <u>K</u>now	What We <u>W</u>ant to Know	What We <u>L</u>earned

Web

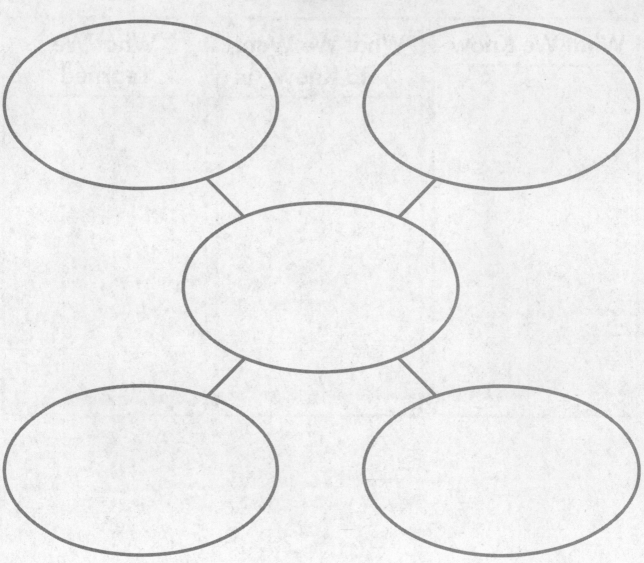

Main Idea and Details

Main Idea

Supporting Detail

Supporting Detail

Supporting Detail

Venn Diagram

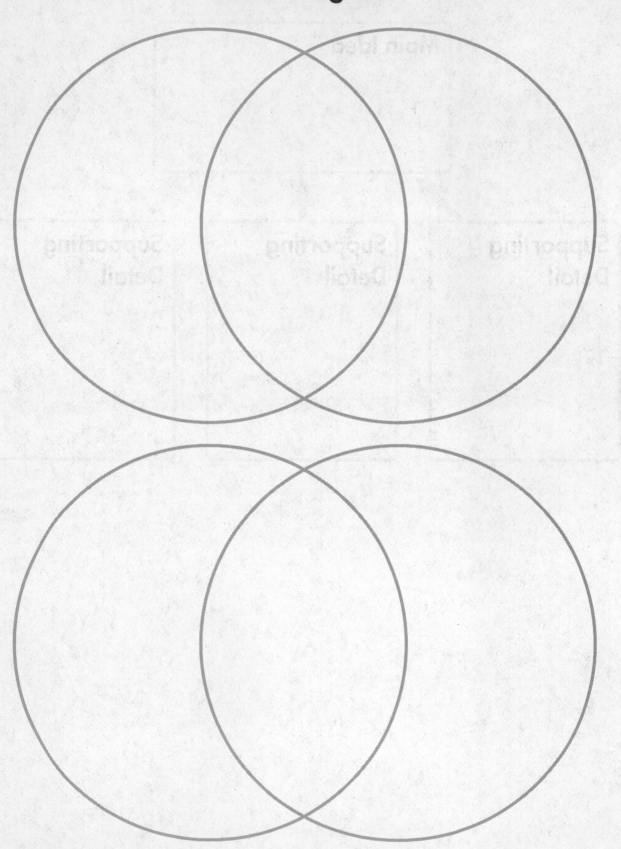

Compare and Contrast

```
┌─────────────────────┐
│ Topics              │
│                     │
│                     │
│                     │
└─────────────────────┘
     ↙           ↘
```

┌──────────────────────┐ ┌──────────────────────┐
│ **Alike**   │ │ **Different**   │
│   │ │   │
│   │ │   │
│   │ │   │
│   │ │   │
│   │ │   │
│   │ │   │
│   │ │   │
│   │ │   │
│   │ │   │
│   │ │   │
└──────────────────────┘ └──────────────────────┘

Cause and Effect

Causes

Effects

Why did it happen?

→

What happened?

Why did it happen?

→

What happened?

Why did it happen?

→

What happened?

Problem and Solution A

Problem

Solution

Problem and Solution B

Problem

⬇

How I Tried to Solve the Problem

⬇

Solution

Steps in a Process A

Process

....

....

Step 1

↓

Step 2

↓

Step 3

Steps in a Process B

Process

....

....

Step 1

Step 2

Step 3

Step 4

T-Chart

Three-Column Chart

Four-Column Chart

Outline Form

Title

....

....

A. ....

    1. ....

    2. ....

    3. ....

B. ....

    1. ....

    2. ....

    3. ....

C. ....

    1. ....

    2. ....

    3. ....

Answer Key

Chapter 1
No answers required for this chapter.

Chapter 2
Quest Activity 1: Making a Budget, p. 22
The handouts should be scored in the following manner:

- Each ship purchased is worth 5 points.
- Each five crew missing from the required total for a full ship is -2 points.
- Each five boxes of food missing from the required total for the number of sailors is -2 points.

Students must meet the threshold for point subtraction in any given category (e.g., if the student is four sailors short of a full ship, no points are deducted).

Quest Activity 2: Hiring Sailors, p. 18
Points can be awarded as follows:
Artwork matching the intent of the ad: 1 point
Effective use of vocabulary: 2 points
Correct spelling and grammar: 2 points

Quest Activity 3: Letters From the Captain, p. 23
Top-left: The Cartographer
Top Right: The Chief Steward
Center: The Patron
Bottom Left: The Navigator
Bottom Right: The First Mate

Quick Activity: Navigational Crossword Puzzle, p. 31
Across: 1. prime meridian 4. latitude 5. sextant 6. longitude
7. John Harrison 8. chronometer
Down: 2. Equator 3. astrolabe

Quick Activity: Finding Coordinates, p. 28
Genoa, Italy: 44.4056° N, 8.9463° E
Bahamas (Nassau): 25.0480° N, 77.3554° W
The White House: 38.8977° N, 77.0365° W
School: (Answers will vary.)
Orcadas Antartic Base: 60.740278° S, 44.7425° W

Note that results may vary slightly depending on type of GPS system or software used.

Chapter 3

Quick Activity: Primary Source: "The New Colossus," p. 51

While answers will vary, students should be able to identify that America is portrayed as a place of hope and promise.

Quick Activity: Comparing Jamestown and Plymouth, p. 52

Students' completed charts should contain some form of the following information:

	Jamestown	Plymouth
Government	First representative legislative assembly in British America.	The Mayflower Compact, a democratic agreement by the colonists aboard the *Mayflower*.
Economy	At first the colony struggled, but began to thrive once tobacco was cultivated on a large scale.	Furs, fishing, lumber, and whale products. Colony was not a large income generator.
Religion	Anglicans (Church of England).	Puritans (separatists from the Church of England).
Social structure (types of settlers, role of women, etc.)	Mostly gentlemen who were not eager to work at first; not many women.	Settlers looking for religious and cultural freedom. Settlers held to strict religious and social codes, especially women.
Geography/ Climate	Hot and humid summers with very cold winters. Usually good weather for farming. Good defensive location.	Warm summers with cold winters. Good harbors, with good fishing spots.

Chapter 4

Quest Activity 4: Canassatego, p. 69

1. A situation in which the Iroquois Confederacy has been taken advantage of by the colonists.

2. Because he trusted Brother Onas.

3. The colonists did not respect Indians or their lands.

Quick Activity: Map of the Slave Trade, p. 70

Students' completed Steps in a Process A graphic organizer should be arranged in the following manner:

Process: Steps in the slave trade
Step 1: Manufactured goods travel to Africa.
Step 2: Enslaved African people are sent to North America.
Step 3: Agricultural products (tobacco, sugar, and cotton) are shipped to Europe.

Quick Activity: Pie Chart of Ethnic Groups, p. 75

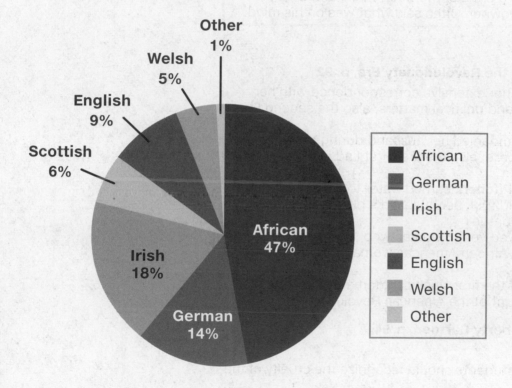

Quick Activity: Salem Witch Trials, p. 76

Students' completed charts should contain some form of the following information:

Tituba	Enslaved woman from Barbados. Told stories that would seem foreign or dangerous to Puritans. May have told fortunes, something Puritans believed to be forbidden by God.
Sarah Good	A homeless woman who muttered to herself when not given food when begging.
Rebecca Nurse	Elderly woman in good standing with the Church. Hard of hearing, and sometimes would not respond when spoken to. Once argued with a Puritan minister over the boundaries of her land.
John Proctor	Was a critic of the witch trials, and a rich landowner. Often said what was on his mind.

Chapter 5

Quick Activity: Women of the Revolutionary Era, p. 92

Abigail Adams: known for her extensive correspondence with her patriot husband on social and political matters; also the second First Lady of the United States

Martha Washington: accompanied her husband during the time the Army spent at Valley Forge; also the first First Lady of the United States

Mary Ludwig Hays (Molly Pitcher): carried water to soldiers during the Battle of Monmouth and took her husband's place at his cannon when he collapsed during battle

Phillis Wheatley: an enslaved young woman who learned to read and write and became the first African American woman to publish a book of poetry

Mercy Otis Warren: one of the first significant female historians who wrote an eyewitness account of the American Revolution

Quick Activity: Sons of Liberty Cartoon, p. 94

1. The Boston Tea Party

2. Answers may vary, but students should recognize the cruelty of the attackers.

3. It is a sign of disrespect to the Stamp Act.

4. Tea

Chapter 6

Quest Activity 3: Checks and Balances Cartoon, p. 110

1. The snake represents the British colonies.

2. The colonies must join or die.

Chapter 7

Quick Activity: Mapping the Trail of Tears, p. 136

Students may draw one of several routes shown:

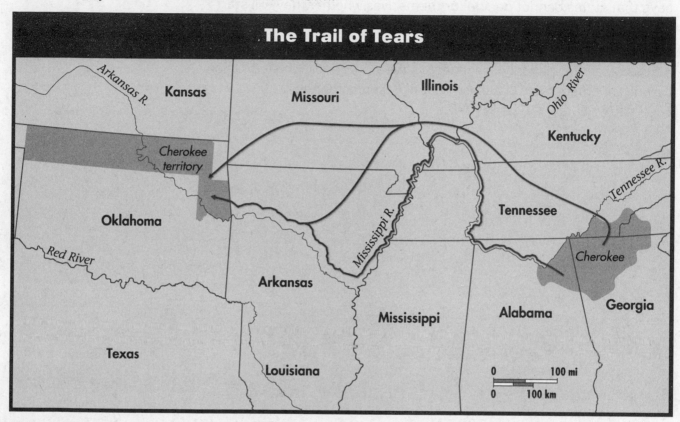

The Trail of Tears

Quick Activity: Lewis and Clark Expedition, p. 138

1. Approximately 3,700 miles (to and from)

2. St. Louis, Missouri

3. Answers will vary but may include references to Oregon Territory and the Pacific Ocean.

Chapter 8

Quick Activity: Comparing Points of View, p. 161

Student answers may vary but should be similar to the following:

1. Wilder: America is the land that farmers conquered and used. Bear: America is the land and the people living on the land.

2. Wilder seems to see land as something to be fought against and overcome, while Bear seems to see land as something with which human beings (specifically American Indians) are united.

Chapter 9

Quest Activity 3: Conventions From the Constitution

Student answers may vary but should be similar to the following:

1. This passage says that only Congress has the power to make rules about territory belonging to the Union, and states do not have that authority.

2. The Declaration of Independence says that anyone unhappy with their government can form their own government, while this passage says that states cannot decide for themselves whether they will start a new government.

Quick Activity: Civil War Crossword

Across: 2. emancipation; 4. secede; 6. impeach; 7. abolitionist; 8. Union

Down: 1. Confederacy; 3. assassination; 5. sharecropper; 7. amendment; 9. Reconstruction

Credits

066: Classic Image/Alamy Stock Photo; 068: Photo
Researchers, Inc/Alamy Stock Photo; 094: Three Lions/
Hulton Royals Collection/Getty Images; 110: Benjamin
Franklin/Library of Congress Prints and Photographs
Division [LC-USZC4-5315]; 118: Niday Picture Library/
Alamy Stock Photo; 137: Illustrated London News Ltd/Mar/
Pantheon/Superstock; 152: National Archives and Records
Administration; 153: Clarence O. Becker Archive/Alamy
Stock Photo; 156: Pictorial Press Ltd/Alamy Stock Photo;
162: Pictorial Press Ltd/Alamy Stock Photo